The World of the Rings

The World of the Rings

Language, Religion, and Adventure in Tolkien

JARED LOBDELL

Open Court
Chicago and La Salle, Illinois

To order books from Open Court, call toll-free 1-800-815-2280, or visit our website at www.opencourtbooks.com.

Open Court Publishing Company is a division of Carus Publishing Company.

This book is a revised edition of *England And Always: Tolkien's World of the Rings* (William B. Eerdmans Publishing Company, 1981).

Library of Congress Cataloging-in-Publication Data

Lobdell, Jared, 1937-
   The world of the rings : language, religion, and adventure in Tolkien / Jared Lobdell.
      p. cm.
   Rev. ed. of: England and always. 1981.
   Includes bibliographical references and index.
   ISBN 0-8126-9569-0 (trade paper : alk. paper)
   1. Tolkien, J. R. R. (John Ronald Reuel), 1892-1973. Lord of the rings.
2. Tolkien, J. R. R. (John Ronald Reuel), 1892-1973—Knowledge—Language
and languages. 3. Tolkien, J. R. R. (John Ronald Reuel), 1892-1973—Religion.
4. Adventure stories, English--History and criticism. 5. Fantasy fiction, English—
History and criticism. 6. Language and languages in literature. 7. Middle Earth
(Imaginary place) 8. Christianity in literature. 9. Religion in literature.
I. Lobdell, Jared, 1937- England and always. II. Title.
PR6039.O32L6353 2004
823'.912—dc22
                                                          2004005613

To H. R. H.
and to my wife
Janice Starke Lobdell

Contents

Foreword
England and Always

For a number of years—say from the days of the first paperback
Lord of the Rings to the very late 1970s—I wondered, in effect,
why no one wrote this book. Paperback printings of *The Lord of
the Rings* numbered fifty or more by the late '70s. Virtually every

bookstore in the United States then had a Tolkien shelf (as indeed, once again, they have one now). And numerous books had even then been written on Tolkien, though not so numerous as now— chief among them, in those days, the authorized biography by Humphrey Carpenter. And yet, excepting Carpenter's book, I could not then find any work on Tolkien giving due weight to the five most obvious facts about the author's life. (Carpenter, who obviously did give consideration to these facts, was, on the other hand, not so much concerned with studying *The Lord of the Rings* as I am here—though from time to time I have quoted from his biography to bolster conclusions I had reached on other grounds. The ideas, if his, are mine also.)

Plainly stated, the five facts are (1) that Tolkien was born January 3, 1892 (in Bloemfontein, South Africa), and therefore grew to manhood in the years before the Great War; (2) that he was a philologist, winding up as Merton Professor of English Language and Literature in the University of Oxford; (3) that he was a Roman Catholic (and devout); (4) that he came from and wrote about the lands in the Northwest of the Old World (most specifically England); and (5) that his *magnum opus* is one of the most successful works of modern times. (This last point, at least, has more recently been recognized by Professor Shippey in his *J. R. R. Tolkien: Author of the Century*.) In what follows I will use these facts as the basis of my inquiry into *The Lord of the Rings*.

I am emphatically not using Tolkien's work as the key to his character. I am not (except very briefly in the fifth chapter) using his character as a key to his work. Either of these might be a worthwhile task—though with C. S. Lewis's disquisition on *The Personal Heresy* in my background I am more than ordinarily skeptical in this area—but neither of them is the task I have undertaken here. What I am hoping to have achieved here is (1) to ask what kind of work Tolkien intended in *The Lord of the Rings* (and to use his primarily Edwardian background as a key); (2) to ask what it is that distinguishes *The Lord of the Rings* from other works in the same genre— whatever genre that may be (and to use Tolkien's professional life as a key); (3) to ask in effect what it all means (using, as might be expected, Tolkien's Catholicism as a key); (4) to ask the significance of the locus of the adventures (what is the value of *North* and *West*); and, finally, (5) to see if these inquiries will reveal what it is about *The Lord of the Rings* that has made it so popular a work.

This approach seemed to me—and still seems—self-evident, though it is true that the fourth chapter has been added since this book was first published. Certainly I can claim no particular credit for having come up with the approach. But perhaps, in the earlier days, the times were not propitious for any endeavor of this sort—as a brief review of some critical history may show. For about a dozen years after *The Lord of the Rings* was first published, the three volumes were a kind of underground success, helped by the praise of such reviewers as C. S. Lewis (in England) and W. H. Auden (in the United States), and a few articles in little magazines. One might call this a success of the catacombs, since it was in considerable part a Christian underground.

From these dozen years came most of the scholars whose work appeared in *Tolkien and the Critics* and *A Tolkien Compass*, as well as some of those, like Clyde Kilby and Paul Kocher, who wrote books on Tolkien. But serious criticism of a cult book with limited circulation suffers from what I might here call the Arthurian Torso syndrome, after C. S. Lewis's study of Charles Williams. There is nothing quite so likely to leave a critic in an excessively exposed position as an attempt to treat a largely unknown and idiosyncratic work as a major achievement. Thus, from 1954 to, say, 1966 circumstances were not favorable for Tolkien criticism.

Then, in the mid-1960s, when the geyser erupted, the new generation of Tolkien fans, concentrated on college campuses, was not quite the same thing as the old. There were holdovers, of course. The University of Wisconsin Tolkien Society, in those days, included scholars of the old order, aficionados of the new, and some who did not fit neatly into either category. But, by and large, the new enthusiasm was of the sort that plays itself out in fanzines and "looks behind *The Lord of the Rings*" and was less likely to produce good literary criticism than to produce the Arthurian Torso sort of enthusiasm. For one thing, Tolkien, having passed into popular culture, seemed to be in danger of passing out of the realm of scholarship—except, of course, the scholarship of popular culture. And scholars of popular culture were unlikely to have a background in philology or even in Catholic doctrine; hence the disinclination of scholars (other than scholars from Christian colleges in the American Midwest) to discuss the themes of *The Lord of the Rings*.

The result was a tendency to talk about Tolkien's work without ever defining what it was—the most obvious and irritating example being the use of the word "trilogy" to describe a six-book, three-decker feigned history that uses the medieval technique of polyphonic narrative to tell what is essentially an adventure story in the Edwardian mode. With so many adjectives or nouns for describing *The Lord of the Rings* more or less accurately it is symptomatic of a failure in criticism that the one word most widely used was just plain wrong.

Wrong also, in my view, or at least misleading, have been a number of other descriptions. Among them, in one respect or another, are "quest" (and this despite Tolkien's own use of the word), "medieval" (except in certain limited ways), and "fantasy" (even in Tolkien's own special sense, and certainly if "fantasy" is used to describe Tolkien's original genre). Now, since these are, next to "trilogy" (or even, in some contexts, more than 'trilogy"), the words most commonly used in connection with *The Lord of the Rings*, it occurs to me that my views may possibly require some justification.

To be sure, there is at least a grain of truth in each description, or the words would not be used as widely as they are. But though the word "quest" in fact appears in *The Lord of the Rings*, the book is not (I would argue) a quest narrative even to the minor degree to which *She* or *King Solomon's Mines* or *The Lost World* are quest narratives. Though the world of *The Lord of the Rings* is medieval in its feel, with its knights and ladies, elves and dwarves, wizards and kings, it is not truly a medieval world: it is virtually without prayer—and besides, if looked at as a medieval world, it shows pronounced anachronisms (Sandyman's new mill, for example, or the entire set of trench-warfare imagery devoted to Mordor). Finally, though "fantasy," especially in Tolkien's definition, seems a word ready-made for *The Lord of the Rings*, the book's Middle-earth is in many ways our familiar world. (This point has been well argued, so far as the return to the Shire is concerned, in an essay by Dr. Robert Plank, in *A Tolkien Compass*.)

Even if we were to conclude that *The Lord of the Rings* could reasonably be called a medieval quest fantasy, I do not believe our conclusion would be particularly useful. We have, in general, only a vague and undifferentiated idea what any one of the three words means, and in fact they do not always mean what readers of Tolkien seem to think they do. The model for a "quest" narrative is the *Queste del Sant Graal*, the search for the Holy Grail.

"Medieval" refers to a period of time in our own history characterized by a particular architecture (Gothic), a particular form of art (manuscript illumination), a certain kind of literature (*contes*), a certain kind of society (feudal), and a certain overriding presence (the church). And "fantasy" (to borrow Tolkien's own definition) refers to a form of literary art combining imagination (the mental power of image-making) with unlikeness to the primary world—that is, with freedom from observed fact. *The Lord of the Rings* is a reverse quest if it is a quest narrative at all: the treasure is to be destroyed, not found. Its Middle-earth is medieval only in its feudal society (even its literature is premedieval). And the book is a feigned history of our world. If Tolkien did, in fact, write a fantasy its name is *Smith of Wootton Major*.

These are not matters central to this book, but I mention them to suggest that my views of Tolkien are to some degree idiosyncratic. To that fact may be traced what some readers will consider an overuse of the first-person singular: I wish to emphasize that what I am saying is my view and not the received or orthodox interpretation. I also wish to give some impression of my own literary travels, both in Tolkien's Middle-earth and in that of such Edwardians as Rider Haggard, Conan Doyle, and the band of scholars who took over Sir James Murray's *New English Dictionary*.

My own travels into Tolkien's world began not with *The Hobbit* or *The Lord of the Rings* but with C. S. Lewis. From the time I first read *Out of the Silent Planet* (in 1951), I had a longing to be part of Ransom's world, and Ransom was a philologist. And from the time I first read *That Hideous Strength* (also in 1951), I longed to read that account of Numinor (so spelled) then existing only "in the MSS of my friend, Professor J. R. R. Tolkien." Thus, when *The Fellowship of the Ring* appeared in 1954, it was on my Christmas list, and I anxiously awaited the conclusion of the story not published until the next year.

Because Lewis was, as I have argued elsewhere, profoundly influenced by the imaginative life of his friends, and especially by Tolkien's imaginative life, his works provide a legitimate—if dangerous—path on which to approach *The Lord of the Rings*. It is legitimate because of the long and close friendship between the two, which lasted more than a quarter of a century and because Lewis, a voracious and retentive reader and listener, created his own Middle-earth much more from what he read and heard than from what he saw in real life around him. (An exception lies in the brilliant delineation of academic politicking in *That Hideous Strength*, but this need not concern us here.) But this path is dangerous because Tolkien was not the only strong influence on Lewis, and the competing influence, Charles Williams, was unlike Tolkien in almost every way: self-taught, a mystic, a magician, a lover of city pavements, heterodox to Tolkien's orthodoxy, an eccentric, quicksilver, and Renaissance man to Tolkien and his late-nineteenth/early-twentieth-century centricity. It would be a serious critical error to mistake Lewis-preaching-Williams for Lewis-preaching-Tolkien.

Nevertheless, to approach Tolkien through Lewis is, in general, to approach him from the inside, so to speak—like approaching the English Romantics through Southey or Leigh Hunt. One may go wrong, but one is likely to be going wrong in the right direction. That this is my approach is the result of my own upbringing, and perhaps I should say a few words on that subject here, since I came to Tolkien after a preparation rather different from that of most Tolkien scholars.

The essential characteristic of that preparation was that I grew up on my parents'—and especially my father's—books. That is, I grew up on Conan Doyle (both Sherlock Holmes and Brigadier Gerard, as well as *The White Company* and *Sir Nigel*); on G. A. Henty; on mystery stories (almost all English and including G. K. Chesterton) brought home from the local library in Ho-Ho-Kus, New Jersey; on *The Wind in the Willows* (and, at an earlier age, on *Winnie the Pooh*); and, eventually, on Lewis. There were other books, of course, not so immediately relevant to our concerns here, and there were books at least as relevant that came along later. But these were central, and what was central about them was their Englishness, not in the technical but in the general sense of that word. A child brought up on Peter Wimsey, Reggie Fortune, Sherlock Holmes, and Father Brown is likely to grow into an Anglophile. A child who adds to these the stories of Étienne Gerard, whose humor depends on French misapprehension of the British character, and stories of the days of the Black Prince—and, by the way, Cheyney's *Short History of England*—will have begun to see England as a place apart. Add in a hundred or so books of G. A. Henty's glorification of the British schoolboy and the mixture is a potent one indeed.

I can say that my experience was like Tolkien's in one respect, at least. I was conscious of England as a separate realm—this other Eden, demi-Paradise—to which I was not native but which I ardently desired. I do not suppose this is quite the same feeling as that of the South African–born Tolkien isolated from ordinary English life as an orphan and a Roman Catholic. He was living in the round green land of England but was not of it; I desired it from afar. Yet both experiences, I think, lead to the perception of an ideal England, which is, of course, part of the magic of *The Lord of the Rings*.

I should make one final point. I was raised in a Christian, and specifically a Protestant Episcopal, household, and I attended an Episcopal prep school. Cranmer's cadences in *The Book of Common Prayer* and the rhythms of the King James Version gave me a love of Elizabethan (or Henrician) style. Church music gave me a love of trumpets and voice. A ceremonial, hierarchical, and sacramental church (though not Professor Tolkien's) accustomed me to ceremony, hierarchy, and the use of outward and visible signs for inward and spiritual characteristics. And above and beyond all this, being a Christian tends to lead one to Christian authors and a sympathy for them. That J. R. R. Tolkien was a Christian there has never been any doubt. That he was a Christian author, I hope my chapter 3 makes clear.

With this background, I find myself attempting this study of *The Lord of the Rings*. In much of what follows I speak with full recognition of the fact that I am suggesting without proof, by indirection, with nothing much to rely on besides my own confidence that I understand *The Lord of the Rings* better than those with whom I disagree—a confidence sometimes shaken and not always a matter of logic. (Note that in what follows I am speaking from *The Lord of the Rings*, not from *The Hobbit*, and especially not from *The Silmarillion* or *Lost Tales*, or *The History of Middle-earth*, which would illuminate some of the concerns of chapter 3, but perhaps in a way distracting us from our task here).

A shortened form of the first chapter was delivered at the MLA Seminar on Tolkien in New York in December 1976, after being vetted by Christopher Tolkien. I wish to thank him for his courtesy in responding to my requests (not only then but over the years since), Tolkien's publishers (and the professor himself) for allowing me to quote from *The Lord of the Rings*, Professor Tolkien also for his kind responses to my inquiries during his life (and for giving me permission to quote him in his remarks and letters to me), Richard West and other members of the University of Wisconsin Tolkien Society, C. S. Lewis for setting me on the road to Tolkien's Middle-earth, and my parents for buying me my first copies of each of the three volumes. None of these is responsible for my views—except, of course, that when these views faithfully interpret Tolkien, the credit is his. In that sense he is responsible for what follows—but only in that sense.

The second, third, and fifth chapters (which appeared as chapters two through four in the original edition) were written straight through for this book in the fall of 1979, when I was first seeking my Ph.D. at Carnegie Mellon University in Pittsburgh. The fourth chapter was written especially for this edition. Over the years I have written and delivered a number of papers on the origins and nature of "fantasy" as Tolkien apparently created it; they are not included here, but are soon to be published separately under the title *The Rise of Tolkienian Fantasy*. Then, perhaps, after that, I will simply go back to reading *The Lord of the Rings* once more, as I first read it fifty years before.

I dedicated an earlier book (*A Tolkien Compass*) to Tolkien's followers, wherever and in whatever guise. This one I dedicate to the memory of his predecessors and especially to Sir Henry Rider Haggard: squire of Ditchingham, farmer, lover of England and of far countries, and inventor of the Shard of Amyntas—to which, more than any one thing else, we owe *The Lord of the Rings*.

—JARED LOBDELL

Pittsburgh, Pennsylvania, December 1979
Elizabethtown, Pennsylvania, December 2002

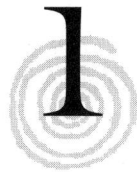

Defining *The Lord of the Rings*: An Adventure Story in the Edwardian Mode

> *We shall not cease from exploration*
> *And the end of all our exploring*
> *Will be to arrive where we started*
> *And know the place for the first time . . .*
> *And all shall be well*
> *And all manner of thing shall be well.*
>
> —T. S. ELIOT, "Little Gidding"
>
> *Beyond the Wild Wood comes the Wide World, said the Rat.*
>
> —KENNETH GRAHAME, *The Wind in the Willows*

It is not at all certain that the game of *Quellenforschung* ("source-hunting") is worth playing with *The Lord of the Rings,* or indeed with most literary creations. Exceptions can be made, of course, for the asking of questions such as "What did Chaucer really do to *Il Filostrato?*" or for the game-playing demanded by *The Waste Land,* but there may well be truth to the suspicion that the game in general is not worth the candle. Yet the search for sources can be part of a search for influences, and the search for influences can be both valid and helpful—as when we look for Vergil's influence on Milton or the influence of the ballads on Coleridge. But we must be looking at both form and subject matter.

Now of course Vergil is an influence on Milton, but is not his source. The influence of the ballads on *The Rime of the Ancient*

Mariner is obvious, but it would be a brave person who considered them Coleridge's sources. Nevertheless, if there were a number of secondary epics that might have influenced Milton, we should, I think, be justified in looking to see which of them served as a source, in order to see which was most likely to have served as an influence. Similarly, if we were interested in finding out which ballads influenced Coleridge, we might well look through the ballad corpus for parallels—sources and analogues—for the *Rime*.

This, essentially, is the kind of endeavor I am engaged in here, in this chapter, for *The Lord of the Rings*. I want to know what kind of work Tolkien set out to write. To which of the great pre-existing forms of literary creation, so different in the expectations they excite and fulfill (the reader may recognize Professor Lewis's words here), so diverse in their powers, is *The Lord of the Rings* designed to contribute? (Lewis 1942, 2). Since even now we do not have available to us any writings in which Professor Tolkien set down an unmistakable answer to that question, and since (despite the intentional fallacy) it is indeed "the first qualification for judging any piece of workmanship, from a corkscrew to a cathedral, to know what it is" (Lewis 1942, 1), I think my endeavor is justified. There may of course be better ways than mine to find out what *The Lord of the Rings* is designed to be, but back in the 1970s this way seemed to be both promising and largely untrod. As even now.

There are two sets of clues to which we should pay particular heed in a search for those whose writing influenced the form of *The Lord of the Rings*, and both sets have been somewhat overlooked. The first set is composed primarily of Tolkien's own comments and secondarily of those few passages in his work where he obviously echoes another author. The second set is composed of the subjective reactions and literary tastes of those readers of *The Lord of the Rings* who have at least a passing familiarity with the English literature of the period in which Tolkien grew up. The first set of clues provides material for answering the question, "Who, according to what Tolkien wrote, may be considered to have influenced him?" The second provides material for answering the question, "Who wrote the kind of book that affects us in the ways *The Lord of the Rings* affects us, and, the dates being right, may therefore have written the kind of book Tolkien would be likely to have read?" (The implicit assumption here is that authors write the kind of book they like to read.)

If we are to make use of both sets of clues, it is of course necessary for us to have some idea of the way Tolkien's mind worked. The continued publication of *The History of Middleearth* through the agency of Christopher Tolkien has provided as much information on this as we are likely to have on any author, but I think he has given me little reason to alter my original (albeit tentative) conclusions. Indeed, I have seen little reason to alter them since I began the quest whose result is this book, some thirty years ago. I thought then, and I think now, that the material published in Professor Tolkien's lifetime at least points the way we should take, and in any case, what I am interested in here is at least as much what went into Tolkien's pot, and what he intended to make of it, as what in fact came out of it. We can begin by quoting Tolkien's reaction to the tale of the juniper tree (J. R. R. Tolkien 1984, 128).

"The beauty and horror" of the tale, he says, "with its exquisite and tragic beginning, the abominable cannibal stew, the gruesome bones, the gay and vengeful bird-spirit coming out of a mist that rose from the tree, has remained with me since childhood; and yet always the chief flavour of that tale lingering in the memory was not beauty or horror, but distance and a great abyss of time, not measurable even by *twe tusend Jöhr*." And, as I hope to demonstrate, we can see in some of Tolkien's other reading the impress of that dark backward and abysm of time.

At the same time, we can see in his childhood reading of dictionaries a fascination with languages. Indeed, his mind was chiefly attuned to languages and the past—which is not, I should emphasize, the same thing as being interested in words and history. I shall have occasion to refer to this again, more than once, but it may be a good thing to mention here Tolkien's reference to the remark of Sjéra Tomas Saemundsson: "Languages are the chief distinguishing marks of peoples. No people in fact comes into being until it speaks a language of its own; let the languages perish, and the peoples perish too, or become different peoples" (1984, 166). The languages are more than the words (for that matter, if I may coin a Yogi Berra-ism, even the words are more than the words). And in the same way the past is more than its history. History is only the facts, or rather a presentation of the facts, accidentally left to us from the past. We cannot get into the real forest of the past; that is part of what the word "past" means.

It must also be made clear that to give the direction of Tolkien's mind is not yet to explain how his mind worked, only to give what mathematicians might call the parameters of its working. The important thing for us to remember here is that, while grammar studies the rules of language, and history studies the rules of the past (one might say history is the grammar of the past), Tolkien's reactions to these things were not those of a grammarian. He said that *The Lord of the Rings* contained "in the way of presentation I find most natural, much of what I personally have received from the study of things Celtic" (quoted in Tolkien 1984a). And he once remarked that his "typical response upon reading a medieval work was to desire not so much to make a philological or critical study of it, as to write a modern work in the same tradition" (West 1980, quoting Eugène Vinaver).

In Tolkien's professional life, as we know, the intersection of language and the past came in the realm of philology. In the inward life of his imagination, it came in his creation of a new version of Middle-earth. There have, of course, been various other versions, from the Midgard of the Norsemen to Langland's fair field full of folk: as Tolkien has reminded us, Middle-earth is not his creation, though he created the "Middle-earth" of *The Lord of the Rings*. That act of creation was necessary before a story could be written about his Middle-earth, but it is the story, and not the creation, that is our subject here.

We know that *The Lord of the Rings* was far from the first story whose events took place within the bounds of Tolkien's Middle-earth. We know also that Tolkien wrote other stories as his children were growing up, and these might repay our attention by giving us additional clues for our endeavor. But I have deliberately left aside from this book any consideration of Ronald Tolkien as his children's father, and thus *Mr Bliss* and *Roverandom*, and even *The Hobbit* and *Farmer Giles*. Let us for now look at our two sets of clues, and what they can tell us about *The Lord of the Rings*.

First, we may look at writers whose influence Tolkien himself acknowledged, or to whose works he referred, or whose works he conspicuously echoed. The list is not long, and the first name on it, Sir Henry Rider Haggard, has some claim to be the most important—though there is an importance also to the Scottish Victorian S. R. Crockett. In a telephone conversation with the American journalist Henry Resnick, Tolkien said this of Haggard's *She*: "I suppose as a boy *She* interested me as much as anything—like the Greek shard of Amyntas, which was the kind of machine by which everything got moving" (in *Niekas* 1967). And, if that were not enough, we have evident parallels between the death of Ayesha (the She of the title) and the death of Saruman. Perhaps it would be well to set them out here.

Haggard's description of the death of Ayesha may be the less familiar of the two:

> Smaller she grew and smaller yet, till she was no larger than a monkey. Now the skin had puckered into a million wrinkles, and on her shapeless face was the mark of unutterable age. I never saw anything like it; nobody ever saw anything to equal the infinite age which was graven on that fearful countenance, no bigger now than a two-months' child, though the skull retained its same size. . . . I took up Ayesha's kirtle . . . and the gauzy scarf . . . and, averting my head, I covered up that dreadful relic." (Haggard n.d. [1888], 222–23)

Beside this may be set Tolkien's description of the death of Saruman: "Frodo looked down on the body with pity and horror, for as he looked it seemed that long years of death were suddenly revealed in it, and it shrank, and the shrivelled face became rags of skin upon a hideous skull. Lifting up the skirt of the dirty cloak that sprawled beside it, he covered it over, and turned away" (III, 370). The parallel is not exact, but it is certainly highly suggestive. Nor do I think it would be stretching a point to bring in, as additional evidence, the importance of caves in both Haggard and Tolkien (though George MacDonald may also be important here, if nowhere else).

In *King Solomon's Mines*, the Don is found dead in a cave on the way, the dead kings are enthroned in a cave, and the travelers very nearly entombed there as well. In *She* the secret fire of immortality, which destroys Ayesha, is likewise in a cave—and, of course, both fire and cave have their parallels in Orodruin. The Mines of Moria, Shelob's lair, all those dark places where "the flowers of symbelmyne come never to the world's end," all testify eloquently to this similarity between Haggard and Tolkien. (Though Freudians may find a different explanation, I prefer mine.) Perhaps it would also be worth recalling here that Haggard was drawn to Africa, where he had been secretary to the Governor of Natal, because of its mystery, its age-old past, and even (though not so strongly) the majesty of its languages. Given this evidence, I think we will not be far wrong if we assign to Haggard a chief place among Tolkien's literary forebears.

Next comes the man who is in many ways the archetypical Edwardian adventure writer, in his Scottishness certainly, and, I would argue, in his technique. I refer to S. R. Crockett, author of *The Black Douglas* (1899). Professor Tolkien has spoken of this not only as Crockett's "best romance" but as "one that deeply impressed me in school days" and goes on to mention that it includes Gilles de Retz as a Satanist and the model for the Necromancer (Tolkien 1981, 391). The implication is certainly that Tolkien, as a schoolboy, read some considerable number of Crockett's romances. The title, by the way, is misleading to anyone who remembers the verse "Hush ye, hush ye, do not fret ye, The Black Douglas shall not get ye"—for that referred to the Douglas who was friend and right-hand man to Robert Bruce, whilst the action of the novel takes place in the mid-fifteenth century, a good part of an hundred and fifty years later.

The story is not told by Sholto McKim, servant to the Black Earls of Douglas (and the Fair Maid of Galloway), but is told as though taken from his memoirs. The Black Douglas is the appellation of the Earls of Douglas (as distinct from the Red Douglas Earls of Angus) in the fifteenth century. The earls, it may be noted, were not long-livers in that time. The story stretches from 1439, when the book opens, in the time of the sixth earl, then a boy of fifteen, approximately to the deprivation of the ninth earl from his earldom in 1455, though the last scene, which I will shortly quote, is indefinitely later. The murderer of the young Earl of Douglas is the Marshal of France, Gilles de Retz, the Bluebeard of history (one of the few historical characters to enter folk or fairy tale, and as Tolkien has told us, the source of his creation of Sauron). The climactic scene is his betrayal by Sybilla and his seizure just as he was to add to his victims the Fair Maid of Galloway and Sholto's beloved. (The Fair Maid of Galloway is likewise an historical character who entered at least into legendary history in Scotland, if not into legend.)

Some idea of the influence of *The Black Douglas* on *The Lord of the Rings* might be gathered from the lines of the text that inspire the illustrations, beginning with the frontispiece ("And at the last he sailed over the seas to his own land"), and including "'I am too young,' he muttered; 'I am not worthy'" (166), as well as "But there cometh a night when every one of us watches the grey shallows to the east for those that shall return no more" (195), and the simple heading "The prisoners of the White Tower" (383). And listen to the last lines of the book:

> This is the end, and yet not the end. For still, say the country folk, when the leaves are greenest by the lakeside, when the white thorn is whitest and the sun drops most gloriously behind the purpling hills of the west, when the children sing like mavises on the clachan greens, you may chance to spy under the Three Thorns of Carlinwark a lady fairer than mortal eye hath seen. She will be sitting gracefully on a white palfrey and hearkening to the bairns singing by the watersides. And the tears fall down her cheeks as she listens, in the place wherein the springtime of the year young William Douglas first met the Lady Sybilla. (479)

Which is not far from our text.

> And there at last, when the mallorn leaves were falling, but Spring had not yet come, she laid herself to rest upon Cerin Amroth, and there is her green grave until all the days of her life are utterly forgotten by men that come after, and elanor and niphrodel bloom no more east of the sea.

Next to Haggard and Crockett—here we may be on more tenuous grounds—we find G. K. Chesterton, between whose works and Tolkien's "On Fairy Stories" we can trace a set of connections, including some Tolkienian passages with a remarkably Chestertonian ring. Let me give you some examples of what I mean. Andrew Lang once remarked that the taste of children "remains like the taste of their naked ancestors thousands of years ago" (quoted in J. R. R. Tolkien 1984, 134). Tolkien began his response by saying, "But do we really know much about these 'naked ancestors' except that they were certainly not naked?" When Max Müller claimed that mythology was a "disease of language" (quoted in J. R. R. Tolkien 1984, 121), Tolkien made this reply: "Mythology is not a disease at all, though it may like all human things become diseased. You might as well say that thinking is a disease of the mind. It would be more near the truth to say that languages, especially modern European languages, are a disease of mythology" 121–22). Either response could have been written by Chesterton: the first, in fact, echoes a passage in *The Everlasting Man*.

Finally, I would challenge readers who do not recognize it to tell me whether Tolkien or Chesterton wrote the passage which is my third example: "We may put a deadly green upon a man's face and produce a horror; we may make the rare and terrible blue moon to shine; or we may cause woods to spring with silver leaves and rams to wear fleeces of gold, and put hot fire into the belly of the cold worm." In fact, this quotation, like the others, is from "On Fairy Stories" (in *The Monsters and the Critics*, p. 122). Nevertheless, we do not know whether Tolkien read the early Chesterton of *The Man Who Was Thursday* or *The Napoleon of Notting Hill*. On the available evidence we can only say that it seems highly likely, and on that basis look briefly at what Chesterton was trying to do, and what it was that he succeeded in doing.

Haggard in ordinary life was a sufficiently prosaic Englishman (an expert on English agriculture) and sought in his books to portray the romance of what everyone could see was romantic. Chesterton, on the other hand, was anything but ordinary, and I think it not coincidental that he sought to portray the romance of what everyone could see was prosaic: "We feel it is epical when man with one wild arrow strikes a distant bird. Is it not also epical when man with one wild engine strikes a distant station?" (2001, 8). Chesterton's paradox can grow wearying, but the root of his love for paradox lies in the unparadoxical belief that the wide world is really a remarkably interesting place after all, and we should remember that. How, then, might this have influenced Tolkien in *The Lord of the Rings*?

Most directly, I believe, in the very character of the hobbits. As Chesterton's Father Brown is short and round and the essence of the Norfolk flats, so Bilbo Baggins is short and round and the essence of an English shire. Perhaps the Battle of Bywater is not unlike the battles in *The Napoleon of Notting Hill*. Of course, it is true that at these points Chestertonian paradox was touching something deep in the paradoxical character of England, and Tolkien could certainly have touched it entirely without Chesterton's intermediation. But I do not think he did.

Fourth among the authors Tolkien read—and here I claim an unfair advantage in the game of *Quellenforschung*—was Algernon Blackwood. The evidence I have seen lies in an entry in the original (but not the edited and published) version of "Notes on the

Nomenclature of *The Lord of the Rings*," in which Tolkien traces his use of "the crack of doom" to a story by Blackwood. Now for our purposes it is unimportant whether the source of Tolkien's Crack of Doom (in Orodruin) was indeed in something Blackwood wrote; what is important is that Tolkien could not have thought it was if he had not read (and been influenced by) Blackwood. I suspect there may be confirmatory evidence for the reading (and the influence) in the character of Old Man Willow, though he is not so terrible as the willows in Blackwood's story by that name.

Blackwood's unnamed narrator writes of the "acres of willows, crowding . . . pressing upon the river as though to suffocate it, standing in dense array mile after mile beneath the sky, watching, waiting, listening. . . . Their serried ranks, growing everywhere darker about me as the shadows deepened . . . woke in me the curious and unwelcome suggestion that we had trespassed here upon the borders of . . . a world where we were intruders, a world where we were not invited to remain." And a little later, "the note of the willow-camp became unmistakably plain to me; we were interlopers, trespassers; we were not wanted. The sense of unfamiliarity grew upon me." Finally (in a passage with Entish—or perhaps Huornish—connotations), "They first became visible, these huge figures, just within the tops of the bushes—immense, bronze-coloured, moving . . . I saw them plainly and noted . . . that they were very much larger than human, and indeed that something in their appearance proclaimed them to be *not human* at all. . . . I saw their limbs and huge bodies . . . rising up in a living column. . . ." (1929, 635–6, 644, 647).

The style is different, of course, and yet I catch here in Blackwood something I catch in Tolkien but few others—perhaps at night in the wildwood in *The Wind in the Willows* also (yet those willows are friendlier). I catch a sense of man (or hobbit) as interloper in the woods, of the trees as sentient entities, and of something neither tree nor human—nor yet, as with Saki, clearly Pan. In another story, "The Glamour of the Snow," I find passages that could be glosses on the experience with Caradhras.

Here the hero of the story (not the same as in "The Willows") "tried to turn away in escape, and so trying, found for the first time that the power of the snow—that other power which does not exhilarate but deadens effort—was upon him. The suffocating weakness that it brings to exhausted men, luring them to the sleep of death in her clinging soft embrace, lulling the will and conquering all desire for life—this was awfully upon him" (1929, 125). And then, as he escapes, "For ever close upon his heels came the following forms and voices with the whirling snow-dust. He heard that little silvery voice of death and laughter at his back. Shrill and wild, with the whistling of the wind past his ears, he caught its pursuing tones; but in anger now. . ." (1929, 127).

I am not suggesting here that Blackwood is Tolkien's source for the character of Old Man Willow or for the snow-storm at Caradhras; he could be, I suppose, but it is not in this that his importance lies. What I am suggesting is that the cast of Blackwood's mind, as revealed in these passages, is surprisingly like the cast of Tolkien's mind. It does not much matter whether the snow at Caradhras comes from Tolkien's Alpine experiences or from Blackwood's. It matters considerably that they saw the snow in much the same way.

Indeed, it matters enough that we should ask what Blackwood was doing in his stories. The answer is that he was creating the modern story of the supernatural—not the pure ghost story of Montague Rhodes James or the story of the undead that found its best-known expression in Bram Stoker's *Dracula*, but the story in which (if I may be forgiven a paradox of my own) nature itself is in a way supernatural. To be sure, Blackwood wrote ghost stories and stories of the undead, and he wrote stories that did not concern the supernatural at all, but what he added to English literature was a sense of mystery and unreliability underlying ordinary things. Blackwood's vision was of the treachery of natural things in an animate world: call it their mystery if you will, but the mystery has a sinister touch.

It is hard for us to re-create any world-view, especially the view of a world in which we have not lived, but there is little doubt that the generations of England who were brought up on Haggard, on Chesterton, on Blackwood—and on Stevenson, Conan Doyle, G. A. Henty, even Saki—were brought up as romantics, in the common sense of that word. While it is not easy to define romanticism in that common sense, we may at least note that ghost stories and stories of the undead make their first appearance in modern English literature with the Romantics, unless of course one wishes to count *Hamlet* as a ghost story. In any case, that these generations, and their romanticism, died in the trenches of the Great War is a truism. Like other truisms, it is both true and overlooked, as it seems to be largely overlooked that Tolkien fought in that war and began his first stories of Middle-earth while convalescing from its effects, back in the Year of our Lord 1915 (but see our Afterword).

It should be emphasized that these Edwardians of whom I am speaking were all of them storytellers. Their poetry—one thinks of Masefield or Kipling—was narrative poetry, even if it was not a narrative of princes and prelates. To a greater extent than in most of Victoria's reign, their natural form of narrative was the short story. (It is worth recalling that only by an exercise of almost undiluted romanticism did Conan Doyle, in *The Hound of the Baskervilles*, succeed in writing a full-length novel about Sherlock Holmes.) But their short stories in many cases, and their novels in some, were installments in a continuing story. I have elsewhere called these Edwardians "world-creators," and I am not sure how important it is that their worlds were created monthly in *The Strand* rather than in the three-decker novels of Trollope's age. After all, Dickens published his novels in parts, but they are still novels, and (*vide* the Baker Street Irregulars) the world of Sherlock Holmes is still one world for all that it was created story by story over the years. The important point is that what were being written—what were being told—were stories.

All this should give an idea, albeit a sketchy one, of what kind of information exists to make up our first set of clues. It must be admitted that the information is not abundant, and subsequent research will doubtless add a smidgin or two—an author here or there. We have Tolkien's own word for it that he was neither as voracious nor as retentive a reader as his friend Lewis, and of course Lewis once wrote to Charles Moorman, May 15, 1959, that "no one ever influenced Tolkien—you might as well try to influence a Bandersnatch" (Lewis 1993, 481). (Someone more adept than I at the intricacies of Carrolliana may know why a bandersnatch would be particularly difficult to influence—or is it merely that it is difficult to do *anything* to a bandersnatch?) Even so, no writer, especially when young, is immune to influences, and it is certainly reasonable for us to use such clues as we have to try to determine who Tolkien's influences were.

Our second set of clues is, alas, equally sparse. One reason for this is that critics (despite Lewis's *Experiment in Criticism*) have not in general addressed themselves to works of literature with the question in mind, "How is this book being read?" Another reason, at least as important when I began this inquiry back in 1975, is that criticism of Tolkien tended to begin *de novo* with Tolkien, just as most criticism of science fiction seemed to begin *de novo* as though no other fiction had ever been written. Some readers may suggest that I fall into the opposite trap, but that is another story, and we shall see. In any case, to the approach to Tolkien *de novo* there have been for more than a quarter-century at least two exceptions that are of use in our inquiry, both of them provided by English critics. The writers they pick as Tolkien's compeers are not the ones that I would pick, but this may only mean that their taste in Edwardian literature differs from mine. Even if they are not entirely on the right track, I am convinced that the track they are on begins from the right place.

Colin Wilson, in his 1974 *Tree by Tolkien*, suggests a relationship between Tolkien and Jeffrey Farnol. Now to say that Jeffrey Farnol is widely overlooked in most histories of English literature is to overstate the notice taken of him, but as Wilson points out, his picaresque novels were enthusiastically circulated among the members of Tolkien's generation. I do not myself believe that Tolkien read the novels of Jeffrey Farnol, but I emphatically do believe that Wilson has read Farnol's novels and Tolkien's three-deckers for much the same reasons.

In a similar vein, Brian Aldiss compares Tolkien to P. G. Wodehouse. Now this is curious. Aldiss is a scholar of science fiction and fantasy, and his discussion of Tolkien occurs in his history of science fiction (1988, 262). Yet for comparison he goes to an author who did not write science fiction (though he may have written fantasy), and who would not generally be considered to place high on a list of "authors comparable to Tolkien." Upon consideration, I can see more reasons than were initially apparent for the comparison—Wodehouse was, after all, a world creator, and of a very English world at that—but linking the two still has a certain oddness to it (and unfairness, as Aldiss notes). Oddness aside, it provides us with the evidence that Aldiss reads Tolkien at least for some of the reasons he reads Wodehouse. My own contribution here may seem to be at least as odd (and at least as unfair).

I might reasonably make a case for the parallel between a certain kind of Tolkienian "scholarship" and the "scholarship" devoted to the arcana of Sherlock Holmes—thus suggesting that some readers turn to Tolkien's Middle-earth for the same reason that others turn to 221B Baker Street. I have already discussed the parallels between Tolkien and Rider Haggard (or some of them), and could easily claim I read one for largely the same reasons I read the other. I could make a similar claim for John Buchan. But I find by self-analysis that—in some moods at least—I read Tolkien as I read Saki (H. H. Munro). That is a fact. What to do with it is a problem.

Presumably I should be able to find an undercurrent of Tolkien's vision in Saki, or of Saki's vision in Tolkien, or else find that I am particularly attracted to the Edwardian world view exemplified by both. For the first, I cannot imagine that Tolkien much enjoyed Saki: their humor, if not poles apart, is at least extremely dissimilar, and Tolkien lacks Saki's cruelty. To be sure, both Saki and Tolkien were Tories of a sort, and my own mind has that cast. But not of the same sort, and I would prefer for the moment to leave that line of thought aside as a possible red herring (or perhaps, in the circumstances, a blue herring?). I suspect that my turning to Saki, Aldiss's turning to Wodehouse, and Wilson's turning to Jeffrey Farnol have in common principally the fact that each of us is turning to the first (or close to the first) Edwardian author with whom we came in contact. I should note here that William Ready (in his badly misnamed *Understanding Tolkien*) observed the Edwardian nature of *The Lord of the Rings*, but he shunned what I welcome, and is in any case a rogue critic in the field. Still, this may be useful as confirmatory evidence.

Those who have followed me thus far make think it also odd, if not remarkable, that I have managed to discuss the sources and analogues of *The Lord of the Rings* without turning to the *Elder Edda* or *Beowulf* or any of the other commonplaces of the discussions frequently heard on the literary genesis of Tolkien's work. But these are properly the subject of another inquiry, I think: they are part of the influence of Tolkien's professional life on his imaginative life. This, by contrast, is a look at the influence of a certain group of imaginative writers of his own time on Tolkien's imaginative life, so far as that influence affects, first, the form of his work, and second, its nature. At least according to the "bandersnatch" theory, the *terminus ad quem* of my inquiry more or less antedates the *terminus a quo* of the other.

I have noted Tolkien's statement that his first response on reading a medieval work was to want to write a modern work in the same tradition. If that was true throughout his life, and not only of medieval works, then it is certainly proper to look at the kind of stories he read to see what kind of stories he was trying to write. From what I know I would argue that in *The Lord of the Rings* Tolkien set out to write an adventure story of the Rider Haggard sort, with overtones of S. R. Crockett and G. K. Chesterton and undertones of Algernon Blackwood, an adventure story in what I call the Edwardian mode. I would like to argue—anticlimax or not—that this "adventure story in the Edwardian mode" was precisely the pre-existing form of literary creation with its own set of expectations to excite and fulfill, and its own diverse powers, that we are searching for. I would like to spend some time in this chapter examining the form, and then the antecedents for the form as Tolkien developed it.

The Edwardian adventure story might be of the "I have before me as I write" sort (to borrow Peter Fleming's phrase), in which a particular object associated with the adventure leads the author into his book. It might be a travel story, beginning with some such phrase as "It's eighteen months or so ago since I first met Sir Henry Curtis and Captain Good, and it was in this way" (Haggard 2002, 7). But however it began, it would, like Conan Doyle's *The Lost World*, be framed in familiarity.

This is, in many ways, the mode of the fairy tale, though we do not always recognize it because the wood choppers and petty kings with which the tales began are, as C. S. Lewis pointed out, as remote to us as the dragons and witches to which the tales proceed (*That Hideous Strength*, Preface). But this is not quite the mode of the fairy tale, for the fairy tale begins "once upon a time," while the Edwardian adventure story begins in rooms in Oxford in the late 1880s, or rooms in Baker Street in the same decade, or with an Edwardian Fleet Street journalist's assignment to interview an eccentric professor, or with an English poet in Saffron Park in the London of the Edwardian age. In economists' jargon, these beginnings are "time-specific."

In this adventure story odd and inexplicable things happen, not in Oxford or Baker Street or Saffron Park, but in the land of the Amahagger, or on Dartmoor, or on a lost plateau in South America, or in a kaleidoscopic adventure across a Europe of enchanted scenery and stock characters—the Europe, one might say, of a dream. In no case is characterization the chief concern of the story. Holly and Job in *She*, Malone and Lord John and Summerlee in *The Lost World*, Holmes and Watson themselves, the Council of Days in *The Man Who Was Thursday*—all are types: the "true but ugly," the "faithful servant," and so on. That they sometimes, as with Holmes, rise to the dignity of archetypes, takes them further yet from the novel of character. (And note, this "archetypicality" is important in our overall inquiry.) In a sense, even if it is a paradoxical sense, in many of these stories it is the character of nature, not the character of any of the actors, that is, as the French would put it, "realized."

That is why Blackwood's "The Willows" follows naturally in the Edwardian mode: there is no real effort at characterization (the author's companion is a stolid Scandinavian), except at the characterization of the willows themselves. And the character that nature bears in these stories is not altogether a good one. (I suspect, by the way of personal aside, that this is one of the things about Saki's work that appeals to me: there is a fey quality to "The Hounds of Fate" and "The Stag" and a thoroughgoing supernaturalism to "Gabriel-Ernest," standing in remarkable contrast to the world of Reginald or Clovis Sangrail. For comparison, one might look to *The Wind in the Willows*—to Badger's house on the one hand, and the Piper at the Gates of Dawn on the other—though I did not and do not care for "The Piper at the Gates of Dawn.")

It should particularly be noted that the adventurers in the Edwardian adventure story are, in general, not solitary. They may be "we few, we happy few," but (if only so that one may tell the story of the other), they are at least two in number—Holmes and Watson, for example. They are likely to be more than two: indeed, the characteristic Edwardian adventure story is that of Sir Henry Curtis, Captain Good, Allan Quatermain, and Ignosi, or of G. E. Challenger, Lord John Roxton, Edward Malone, and Professor Summerlee—the band of (very different) brothers. The narrative is in the first person, even if it involves that first person's bringing in parts of the story of which he had no firsthand knowledge. There is a convention that the story should be told by those whose story it is. In general, the narrator is the most ordinary member of the band of adventurers (Allan Quatermain, Edward Malone, John H. Watson), and the tone of the narration tends to be self-deprecating.

This tone, and the first-person narration, mark the Edwardian mode as something quite apart from the mode of the fairy tale or (*pace* Edmund Wilson) from the school story—though the school story does perhaps represent a separate but related development from the Victorians, and though one continuing school story has recently asserted its place in the realms of fantasy. I think this Edwardian mode of adventure story had its origin in the travel journals and first-person newspaper accounts that were conspicuous features of the English (and American) literary landscape in the second half of the nineteenth century. The names of Richard Burton and H. M. Stanley come immediately to mind, followed by the war correspondent W. H. Russell and the American John Lloyd Stephens, whose various *Incidents of Travel* books are among the finest examples of this Victorian literature of exploration. It should, however, be pointed out that the self-deprecating tone comes in later, and may have its origins in the tradition of the *pukka sahib*—British understatement, stiff upper lip, and all that— which is in part the legacy of the Duke of Wellington and others who helped establish British India. In any event, in this respect also the Edwardian adventure story would appear to be a case of art imitating life.

One could, I suppose, distinguish between this original travel literature and the derivative literature of Rider Haggard or Conan Doyle, on the grounds that one is more interested in the travelling and the other in what lies at the end—the object of the quest— thus making *King Solomon's Mines* or *She* into a quest story. But I am not sure this would be profitable. The Edwardian adventure story was indeed a story of Englishmen abroad in the wide and mysterious world, but what they were looking for was not so much the Holy Grail or the Golden Fleece as—whatever excuse may have been provided by Maple White or the Shard of Amyntas—the wide world itself. (It is worth noting that the best of Blackwood's stories take place on the Danube or in Canada, or in the Alps.) And it seems that this parallels *The Lord of the Rings*: it does not seem to me that Frodo sets out on a quest much more than Bilbo set out on one in *The Hobbit*. Certainly Frodo and Bilbo, though hobbits, are Englishmen, and to them the "back again" in the subtitle of *The Hobbit* is as important as the "there."

As I have said, the actors in the Edwardian stories were stock Englishmen, most of them. Mostly they returned to England and their workaday lives, if they survived at all. It is not my purpose here to point out in detail how *The Lord of the Rings* conforms to this Edwardian mode, only to suggest its conformity, but perhaps another example of that mode would not be amiss. An example that comes quickly to mind—though the book itself comes after the Edwardian age, having appeared in 1923—is John Buchan's *Huntingtower*, in which the character of the Scottish businessman is so Tolkienian that one would almost assume Tolkien took time off from *The Year's Work in English Studies* to read Buchan. (I owe an initial suggestion along this line to my friend, Mr. J. D. M. Zincavage.) Buchan, admittedly, was Scottish, while the Shire is "forever England"—but that is not an insuperable difference, any more than Crockett's Scottishness.

The quite ordinary Englishmen (or, occasionally, Scots or Irishmen) who set off on their travels in these Edwardian adventure stories do more than merely see strange sights and have strange adventures: they sense a mysterious character indwelling in the world itself, or at least in that part of the world in which the adventures take place. The story may be of their triumph over nature (as with *The Lost World*), or it may be of their escape from it ("The Willows"). It may be, in later and lesser form, a story of romance and a mysterious Russian princess (as in *Huntingtower*). Or the mystery may be—and frequently is—that of the past mysteriously alive in the present. This is the case with *King Solomon's Mines*, *She*, *The Lost World*, much of Chesterton, and the very idea of the ghost story, whether by Blackwood or M. R. James or whomever.

In fact, from the number of examples I can call to mind, this might be taken as a hallmark of the Edwardian mode. To be sure, others have felt the lure of the past: it is a part of the nature of romanticism, and it was a Victorian, not an Edwardian, who wrote (if he wrote nothing else worthwhile) the great line "A rose red city half as old as time." But the past alive in the present in a recurring motif in the Edwardian adventure story nonetheless.

The framework of the story, even in Haggard's time, is "there and back again." The "back again" is skimped, and it would appear, in part, a convention necessitated by the first-person narrative: the narrator has to return home in order to tell his story (though Haggard did find a way around this in *She*). By Blackwood's time—as a result, I suppose, of the short-story form—the framework largely disappears, and we are left with the real kernel of the story, which in Blackwood is the mystery (or the "supernaturalism") of nature. (Chesterton dropped the first-person narrative, while retaining the view of the first-person narrator, who likewise must return home to tell the story.)

It may be objected that I have taken three disparate authors and parceled them together very oddly, and that an "Edwardian mode" that overlooks Baron Corvo on the one hand or Henry James on the other is scarcely worth discussing seriously. Now I could look at either of these and find something of the sense of the past I have been discussing here, just as I could find it in Bram Stoker. But what have I, or Tolkien, to do with feigned autobiography in the manner of *Hadrian VII* or novels of character in the manner of *The Ambassadors*? The ancestry of the adventure story in this Edwardian mode is the line from which comes much of Tolkienian "fantasy," and it is to be found in Scott, perhaps the Dickens of *A Tale of Two Cities*, in Burton and Stanley, in Stephens, and especially in that novelist of wilderness adventure, Fenimore Cooper—the list is very long. This Edwardian adventure story has its late Victorian affinities with G. A. Henty, and as in Henty's novels, where boys who make their way without benefit of birth are frequently found to have had that benefit all along (but were stolen or orphaned as very young children), the Edwardian adventure story is frankly aristocratic in its conventions—as was the Edwardian world from which it came.

That *The Lord of the Rings* is an exemplar of this Edwardian mode is at the root of the adverse reactions by such readers as William Ready or Edmund Wilson. In a way—and here Mr. Aldiss is correct—its basic presuppositions are those of P. G. Wodehouse, though Tolkien's knowledge of political reality was far superior to Wodehouse's. (On this point see Dr. Robert Plank's "The Scouring of the Shire" in *A Tolkien Compass*.) I am not here concerned with the literary value of Edwardian adventure stories (except to note that Lewis's test in *Experiment in Criticism* should convince us they have one). But Tolkien's adverse critics have in fact been concerned with that value, to the extent of denying that it exists.

I am not here concerned with such questions as whether the aristocratic—or the Tory—view of things is the right one. But Tolkien's adverse critics have in fact been concerned with that question, and have given an unequivocal answer, unequivocally expressed. What the adverse critics have not been concerned with is my concern here: using my scattered evidence on sources to find out what kind of work Tolkien is likely to have been writing, and therefore (to some degree) what kind of work he wrote.

Certainly this adventure story in the Edwardian mode is a prime candidate to be considered the pre-existing form to which *The Lord of the Rings* was designed to contribute. At the very least, a formal comparison of *The Lord of the Rings* with other exemplars of the mode should prove to be enlightening. While not making the formal comparison here (finding the road is sometimes more fun than taking it), I might suggest the lines along which it could be made. Take Conan Doyle's *The Lost World* as an exemplar.

In this story the four travelers come together more or less by accident—or by the machinations of Professor Challenger (who is not with them for the entire journey). *The Lord of the Rings* has, of course, nine travelers, who come together more or less by accident—or partly by Gandalf's intent (and Gandalf does not make the entire journey with them). The four travel to unknown lands, seeking a way up (and then a way down) a mysterious plateau—involving, on the way down, travel through a cave. The Nine Walkers likewise travel to unknown lands, with Frodo and Sam seeking a way up (through Shelob's cave). The four are types: sportsman, Irish rugger, desiccated (but tough) professor, and the eccentric omnicompetent. The Nine likewise are types: master and man, enthusiastic but fallible assistants, warrior, king-in-exile, elf, dwarf, and the eccentric omnicompetent, Gandalf—though he is far more pleasant than G. E. Challenger.

Further parallels are easy enough to discover. Nature—in the form of prehistoric animals and even (perhaps) the ape-men—attacks the four. Nature—in the form of Old Man Willow or the snow at Caradhras—attacks the Nine. The four come safely through to the triumph; eight of the Nine Walkers do likewise. The story of the four is told by the most "ordinary" of the group, Edward Dunn Malone (but, ordinary or not, "there are heroisms all around us"). Similarly, the story of the Nine is told by Frodo, whom Professor David Miller has called the "common lens for heroic experience"—ordinary on the surface, but not beneath it. (Admittedly, it is told from the books compiled by Frodo—rather than directly by him—but the point remains the same.) The very attraction of the lost world is the past alive in the present on the mysterious plateau. And certainly the continually sounding theme of *The Lord of the Rings* is the past alive in the present: the Ring, Gandalf, Galadriel, Elrond, the sword reforged, the Barrow Wights—to list examples is to list nearly everything in the book.

I have elsewhere suggested (in a review of *The Lord of the Rings* many years ago in *The Libertarian Review*) that after the Great War there was a division in the Edwardian inheritance between the storytellers and the world re-creators—between Edgar Rice Burroughs and Angela Thirkell, the pulp writers and the country-house novelists. One might almost say the division was between those who were chiefly interested in the "there" and those who were chiefly interested in the "back again." I still think that this is true, and that, as I also suggested, Tolkien brought the long-sundered branches of the Edwardian line back together again—for which reason he, more than P. G. Wodehouse, deserved the title of "the last Edwardian." But I am not sure how much emphasis this merits here. Though the Shire's Tory quality is unmistakable, its idylls include no country houses, and my present concern is not so much with the Edwardian inheritance, as with the Edwardian mode of *The Lord of the Rings*—with the fact that Tolkien was writing an Edwardian adventure story.

It may be introduced as an objection that the Edwardian mode tended at least toward shorter novels, and in its final form toward the short story. Moreover, the speed of its writing, as well as the pace of its action, was almost journalistic. Haggard wrote *King Solomon's Mines* in six weeks, and Conan Doyle cranked out Sherlock Holmes at high speed for monthly publication. Chesterton wrote prodigiously, hastily—one might say, gargantuanly. But Tolkien wrote a three-decker novel, and took forty years to write it, if one counts from his beginning *The Silmarillion*, or twenty-five years, if one counts from the time he began the story of Bilbo Baggins. But I think we would find that the variation in the basic form represented by *The Lord of the Rings* was determined by his professional life, and its gestation time determined the same way.

That is to say, what differentiates Tolkien from other writers of Edwardian adventure stories generally would be properly treated in a discussion of the influence of his professional life on his imaginative creation, with the root of the difference lying in the love of language that led him to philology as his life's work. But that, as Aristotle taught us the formula (long before Kipling), is another story. It is the story of the philologist's world, and not the Edwardian mode, of *The Lord of the Rings*. To write it requires some knowledge of what a philologist does and how his mind works, and the writing has been very well done by Professor T. A. Shippey. To write what I have written here so far has required only a knowledge of what it was Tolkien read in the first ten years of this century, or may have read—a far easier requirement, and made easier yet for me by the fact that I was brought up on the same books. To me this game of *Quellenforschung* has been a game of auld acquaintance, and doubly enjoyable on that account. I hope it has been instructive to the reader besides being entertaining to me. And its value, I think, is clear.

We will be armed against a tendency to attack (or defend) Tolkien—or his creation—on the wrong grounds if we can determine what the proper grounds are—that is, what *The Lord of the Rings* is intended to be. And in that intent is, I think, the key to the creation of what we now call fantasy. To go back for a moment to Professor Lewis's example, it is necessary to know what the corkscrew or the cathedral is designed to do before we can say it is well- or ill-designed: once we know what the purposes are, the prohibitionist may attack the corkscrew or the Communist attack the cathedral. And here it is important to realize one thing: the attack of the prohibitionist or the Communist is not an attack on the corkscrew or the cathedral for failure to work according to plan. The better the corkscrew works, the less the prohibitionist will like it. The more people pray in the cathedral, the more the Communist will seek to shut it down. The greater the success of *The Lord of the Rings* as an adventure story in the Edwardian mode, the more those who dislike adventure stories in the Edwardian mode will seek to denigrate and depreciate it.

In part the critical dislike of this mode is merely an example of the critical dislike of adventure stories of all kinds, a point which Professor Lewis illustrated in his essay "On Stories" and which I need not illustrate here. But the dislike runs deeper for this mode than for others, and I suspect that there are those who enjoy *Don Quixote* or *The Three Musketeers* (or *The Man in the Iron Mask*) who do not enjoy the Edwardian adventure story any more than they enjoy the *Chanson de Roland*, with its good Christians and bad infidels ("Païens ont tort et Chrestiens ont droit"). The different modes of the adventure story appeal to somewhat different—perhaps very different—audiences, and it would be a mistake not to distinguish among these modes. It would particularly be a mistake when it is this mode that, through Tolkien's creation of *The Lord of the Rings*, has been the fount and origin of modern ("Tolkienian") fantasy.

The particular characteristics of the Edwardian mode that seem to cause the most trouble for the critics are those that apparently form the substratum of almost all popular Edwardian literature: the aristocratic view, the black and white morality, the lack of interest in character development (certainly more extreme in this mode than in others), the movement of "there and back again," the emphasis on "we few, we happy few" (related to, but not altogether the same as, the aristocratic view), the fascination of the past alive in the present, the undercurrent of mystery (or even malignity) in nature. On the other hand, if one looked at the chief forms of the adventure story in the latter part of the twentieth century and beginning of the twenty-first, he will find not these but the morally ambiguous: the hard-drinking and hard-wenching private eye, the solipsistic James Bond, the not-so-good sheriff and not-so-bad outlaw. If all these are part of the current mode of the adventure story, we could reasonably expect to find the Edwardian mode disliked. (But, of course, now, in 2004, through Peter Jackson and his film, our observer looking at the chief forms of the adventure story will also find *The Lord of the Rings*.)

Now the evidence of Colin Wilson and Brian Aldiss (and in conversation I have found others who support his linking of Tolkien and Wodehouse), as well as my own aberration toward Saki and the world of Clovis Sangrail, should make it clear that there are some readers who enjoy the Edwardian character of *The Lord of the Rings*, for all that Wilson seems perhaps a little uncomfortable in his position and Aldiss speaks of "the counterfeit gold of an Edwardian sunset" (1988, 262). But we must be careful not to claim greatness for Tolkien merely because we are enamored of the Edwardian mode, just as those who dislike it should be careful not to deny him greatness because they are not so enamored. And yet, I can hear my readers saying to themselves, "This is all very well, but how can he speak of the Edwardian mode of the adventure story in the same terms in which Lewis spoke of something so beyond it as the secondary epic? Surely it is a little odd to speak of Tolkien in terms that have been reserved for Vergil or Milton. Surely he has lost his sense of proportion." A brief explanation may serve to allay such misgivings, though something else I have to say may raise them again, *fortiter in re*.

For the explanation: it may indeed be the case that an epic is a greater thing than an adventure story; this does not mean that a given epic is greater than a given adventure story—and I could also point out that Milton's "Epic following Nature" is very like an adventure story. Perhaps it would be well to note this as a corrective to the view that an adventure story is an inferior thing. Moreover, if a critical system is well drawn up, it should be applicable not only to Vergil and Milton but to the writers of three-deckers (let us say, Tolkien and Trollope) as well. And there remains the corrective supplied in Professor Lewis's *Experiment*: if the work is capable of "good" reading, and most especially of rereading, then we had best be wary of dismissing it out of hand, or indeed at all. After all, popular literature (*vide* Shakespeare in his age) is not necessarily bad, and there is a genuine critical approach embodied in the assertion, "I don't know much about art, but I know what I like." And now for what is likely to raise greater misgivings.

Admittedly, we may be too close in time to *The Lord of the Rings* to judge its place in literary history, even as we are apparently not close enough in time to see what it is supposed to be. On the first (and here is my outrageous suggestion), I think it entirely possible that *The Lord of the Rings* is the last great book that will be read as the great books of old were read, for the story and as a lens through which to view our experience—so that it is indeed important to know what it is and what made it that way. On the second, we know that Tolkien disliked the idea that anyone might write a critical study of his work while he was alive, both because he was a private man not welcoming fame and because he thought it wrong that someone should spin theories about what he had written without checking those theories with him. One appreciates his point, but one also recognizes that it has made criticism of his work more difficult: just as one would have enjoyed a talk with Lewis's ancient Athenian, if not his dinosaur, one would like to have spoken with the last Edwardian.

More may be recovered than I have recovered here. Haggard and Crockett and Chesterton and Blackwood were not the only

authors the young Tolkien read, and Wilson and Aldiss are not the
only critics to have examined Tolkien's work in ways useful for this
kind of endeavor. But with even these few, there is enough evidence to show that *The Lord of the Rings* is an adventure story in
the Edwardian mode, and to justify looking at what went into that
mode. And whether we believe it to be as sublime as the cathedral,
or as mundane as the corkscrew, or somewhere in between in
merry Middle-earth, it should be worth something to us to have
some idea what it is.

The Philologist's World of
The Lord of the Rings

By the delicate, invisible web you wove—
The inexplicable mystery of sound.

—T. S. ELIOT, "To Walter de la Mare"

Bright is the ring of words
When the right man rings them.

—R. L. STEVENSON, "If This Were Faith"

Tolkien began work on *The Silmarillion* while recovering from
the trench fever he contracted during the Great War. But he first
achieved prose publication in quite a different genre (if indeed
"prose" and "genre" are the right words here): in his glossary of
Middle English published in 1922, and in his reports on current
scholarship for *The Year's Work in English Studies* in the years
immediately following. To these may be added his work on the
New English Dictionary (now better known as the *OED*) in 1919
and 1920. The founder of that great achievement, Sir James
Murray, had died a few years before, his work unfinished but his
goal in sight—a complete dictionary of the English tongue on
historical principles, following each word in all its changes
through time, from the time of its first recorded usage to the
present day (or, in this case, the 1920s). Tolkien was one of the
young scholars appointed to finish the task in the years after the
war.

It probably need not be pointed out here that the construction of a dictionary on historical principles is a scholarly version of the effort to see (or define) the past alive in the present. What may need to be pointed out is the immensity of the task that James Murray set for himself (and, much later, his assistants). It took almost six decades from beginning to end (if, indeed, it has ended yet), and six decades was a short time for what was accomplished.

But calling attention to its immensity is paying only half the tribute due. The long unfolding of the English language from *Beowulf* (or even before) to the present day is a great story. The whole panoply of the Indo-European tongues, spread out through space and time over the whole world and six millennia, is one of the greatest stories ever told. And Murray—and those who came after—were caught up in its greatness.

Languages, of course, obey certain laws defining or describing their modification over time, and they obey these laws, generally speaking, in all times and all places, regardless of the separate genius of the language. Whether it is *holbytla* becoming *hobbit* or *kud-dúkan* becoming *kudúk* (to take examples from *The Lord of the Rings*), whether it is *perawa-mes-enki* becoming *peramessing* and then *paramus* (this is Algonquian) or *generalis* (Latin) becoming *geral* (Portuguese), the words wear down. So, too, does the structure of the languages. They begin by being highly inflected—verbs with different forms for each person of a whole array of moods and tenses, nouns with different forms for each of many numbers and cases. There is an old story to the effect that members of certain tribes count "one, two, three, many" (which sounds simple), and then have a different form of the noun involved for each of the four numbers (which is not simple at all). There may be misunderstanding or misreporting here—but we know that even Greek preserves at least a dual. Latin preserves seven different cases—nominative, accusative, genitive, dative, ablative, locative, and vocative—and more tenses and moods than we commonly think of. By contrast, English has worn down much more—in part because Latin was artificially reclassicized in the Renaissance. Indeed, English preserves an elaborate conjugation only in the verb "to be" (and, if anyone should ever use it, the verb "to wit").

Moreover, languages grow more abstract over time. Tolkien turned Max Müller's dictum on its head, but both acknowledged, indeed proclaimed, the connection between language and mythology—and specifically between a young language that denotes many gods and spirits, in ash and oak and thorn, sunrise and sunset, morning and evening star, and where there is yet no word for God any more than there is for "tree." (We will see more of this later.) Only with abstraction can there come such fields as philosophy, theology, or, indeed, literary studies. One cannot discuss "God" with a speaker of a young language: the ancient unities of the language have not yet been broken apart.

Not only do languages change "on their own" (so to speak), but they borrow one from another. One can follow the movement of words from language to language, and thus the movement of the things or ideas they represent from place to place. That approach to language has been one of the keynotes of philology for the last hundred years, and it can be found, suitably adapted, in the appendices to *The Lord of the Rings*. It is a kind of antiquarianism, perhaps, or a kind of genealogy of words (and things); the important thing to be noted here is that this too is a version of the past alive in the present.

Here, to understand what language meant to Tolkien, it may be appropriate to appeal to a book that was never written—the collaboration by Tolkien and C. S. Lewis, *Language and Human Nature*, announced for 1949 publication by the Society for the Promotion of Christian Knowledge. The argument in that book, so far as we can reconstruct it, began with the proposition that all humans have a native language of their own—at least potentially. That language of their own may be no more than giving a personal twist to the shape of old words; it may be the invention of new words (on received models, as a rule); or it may come to the elaboration of a language of their own in private (in private only because other people are not as a rule very interested). To be sure, it is scarcely possible to escape the influence of the inherited first-learned language—those who speak English as a first language speak it *and other languages* differently from those with, say, Urdu or French or Zulu as a first language—and even later-learned languages affect the natural style, coloring one's linguistic taste, if nothing else. But, even so, there are still individual languages, entirely separate languages (invented languages) in some cases, and in others highly individual expressions in the common language: in my own case, I know that if I think I have expressed something perfectly, that is time to beware of others' misunderstanding.

And if one found oneself in voiceless regions where there was nothing like our human language, one's own native language would bubble up and make new names for strange new things. Now, language properly so called, as we know it on Earth—*token* (perceived by sense) plus *significance* (for mind)—is peculiar to an embodied mind: an essential characteristic, the prime characteristic of the fusion of incarnation. Language is therefore connected with our incarnation, and is in some sense the defining characteristic of humankind as *animal rationale*. Only such *animales rationales* (the *Hnau* of Lewis's *Out of the Silent Planet*) would have language. The irrational could not and the unembodied either could not or would not. There is some evidence that Tolkien considered it possible that at least one language existing in historic times might have to some degree preserved an ancient language of humans (would it be Anglo-Saxon, perhaps, having some particular relation to the language of Atlantis—as with Earendil?).

But in their book, I believe, Lewis and Tolkien would have been speaking not merely to the subject of "language and human nature" as involving different languages and different natures (like the "Genius and Genius" of Lewis's early article, or Tom Bombadil as the *genius loci* of Oxfordshire with his language showing his particular nature—as that of the *ŷrch* shows theirs). Their concern was much deeper, and more unitary. Language as we understand it—token and significance—is the mark of the human: to speak a language translating symbol into meaning is to be human, to have a human nature. There is no certainty (whatever Tolkien's speculations) that any or all of our existing languages would be directly derived from the prototype: the only undoubted common inheritance would be the aptitude for making words, even the compelling need to make them.

Note that the prototype language would not be the same as the prime language of other differently constituted rational animals, or of spirits, including angels. If the embodiments are different, the physical basis, which conditions the symbol-forms, would be *ab origine* different. The mind-body blends would have quite different expressive flavors. Without symbols we have no language; and language begins only with incarnation and not before it.

The book would have been consistent with recent hypotheses suggesting that the process of original language-formation is in fact mythopoeic, in a sense defined by anthropologists at the

University of Chicago a half-century and more ago (and not greatly different from what Owen Barfield might have said). In this formulation, a *name* is a force within a person propelling him in a certain direction. In the words of the *Enuma Elish* (going back to the third millennium BCE), there was a time "When no god whosoever had appeared; / Had been named by name, had been determined as to his lot, / Then were gods formed within them [within the primal forces of chaos]." Five millennia ago (in our calendar), it was an immemorial truth that the naming of something was what brought it into existence (or immediately accompanied its being brought into existence) and that the names of gods (or things) expressed their true nature. Quite possibly, cave paintings at the Chauvet caves in France and ivory figurines in the (contemporaneous or even earlier) caves in southwestern Germany give us a date for the invention of language in our Middle-earth, thirty thousand years (or more) before the time of the *Enuma Elish*.

This may seem to be venturing into a byway, but I think not: I think Tolkien's view on language formation was fully in tune with recent developments in anthropology, as his views on Finn and Hengest, for example, anticipated recent developments. These works of art (or sets of works) connected with the hunt and thus arguably religious in nature, date to about 35,000 BCE—the point when, it has been argued, human speech begins. This date almost assumes separate invention of languages (though one would be the first), rather than diffusion from a single source—in other words, the situation imagined for Mars in Lewis's *Out of the Silent Planet*. It is possible to consider both pictures and figurines as the nouns of a spoken language that as yet had only verbs or interjections. A parallel (at the risk of falling into the easy identification of ontogeny and phylogeny) would be with little boys playing with soldiers, telling the story by moving the soldiers and speaking with interjections and perhaps occasional verbs.

It is possible to consider the paintings as full narrative, comprising verbs and nouns, for a people using only interjections (perhaps with dependent modifiers). They would represent adjuncts to language (perhaps even most *of* the language) for peoples in very early language-states. Any history of art will tell us that the paintings and figurines are known to be in some sense "religious"—the explanation would be that they come at this point in human development where religion and speech must be inexplicably intertwined. On this showing, various sets or tribes or peoples would have developed different languages as each inhabited a separate *koinosphere* (world where language became possible—became, as one recent theorist has put it, within reach of a leap into the "Adjacent Possible"). But one would have been first. And the existence of the *koinosphere* defines the presence of the human.

So the relationship of language and human nature is twofold. First, the creation of language defines human nature; and second, languages are the chief distinguishing marks of peoples. Those who have read the appendices to *The Lord of the Rings* will recall Professor Tolkien's discussion of the problems of translation (in appendix F): The

> whole of the linguistic setting has been translated as far as possible into terms of our own times. . . . Translation of this kind is, of course, usual because inevitable in any narrative dealing with the past. . . . But I have gone beyond it. [My] procedure perhaps needs some defense. It seemed to me that to present all the names in their original forms would obscure an essential feature of the times as perceived by the Hobbits[:] . . . the contrast between a widespread language, to them as ordinary and habitual as English is to us, and the living remains of far older and more reverend tongues. All names if merely transcribed would seem to modern readers equally remote: for instance, if the Elvish name *Imladris* and the Westron translation *Karningul* had been left unchanged. . . .

And, similarly, the linguistic procedure by which the language of Rohan has been made to resemble ancient English speech "does not imply that the Rohirrim closely resembled the ancient English . . . in culture or art, in weapons or modes of warfare, except in a general way due to their circumstances: a simpler and more primitive people living in contact with a higher and more venerable culture, and occupying lands that had once been part of its domain" (footnote, appendix F). What is and is not to be translated further, in translations of *The Lord of the Rings*, is of course set out in Professor Tolkien's "Notes on the Nomenclature of *The Lord of the Rings*" in *A Tolkien Compass* (Lobdell 1975 and 1980).

I have sometimes thought that it would be an interesting experiment to ask a group of literary scholars, "What major modern work of fiction has as one of its heroes Banazir Galpsi?"—and wait to see how many of them (even the Tolkien scholars among them) would recognize Samwise Gamgee. (A similar question involving Kalimac Brandagamba—that is, Meriadoc Brandybuck—might not be quite so puzzling.) My point is not that the name of Banazir Galpsi is necessarily unfamiliar to Tolkien aficionados (it well may not be) but that the whole world of *The Lord of the Rings* as we perceive it is an English world, indeed a medieval English world, where Elves are Welsh and Dwarves are Norse, both being proper neighbors for this England. (It is true that the Elvish language has Finnish analogues as well, and Dwarvish sounds Middle Eastern, but the point holds nonetheless.) Professor Tolkien himself, as we have noted, referred to *The Lord of the Rings* as a work in which he had incorporated much of what he personally had learned from the study of things Welsh: this "Welshness" of the Elves, like the "Northernness" of the Dwarves and the "Old Englishness" of the Rohirrim, is not imaginary. The Northwest of the Old World in the Third Age is clearly the Northwest of the Old World today— the British Isles. We shall see (somewhat) in chapter 4 what other things it may be.

Much of all this, according to the author, is a matter of translation. The paradox is that the translation is what attracts us. It is because we are reading about Sam Gamgee of the Shire, not Ban Galpsi of Sîza, that we read on. It is not only the familiarity of the language and surroundings that we welcome, but their English familiarity. And yet by Tolkien's feigned history we are reading about what are, to us, prehistoric times (by C. S. Lewis's syncretistic reading, preglacial epochs—which fits in nicely with the Chauvet caves). We may be reading about England, if by England we mean a geographic area, but it is not England in any other sense: the illusion that this is "really" England, as we know it now or in our history is an illusion of translation, as I noted. But as I also noted, the illusion is more real than what underlies it, or is feigned to underlie it.

There is an explanation for this—indeed, two explanations. One is found in the passage I quoted from Sjéra Tomas Saemundsson: "Languages are the chief distinguishing marks of peoples." The language, that is (as in *Language and Human Nature*), defines the nature of its speakers. Thus the "Welshness" of the Elvish language means that the Elves themselves take on Welsh characteristics. The fact that the names of the Dwarves are taken from the *Elder Edda* provides a Northernness for the character of the Dwarves. When Gandalf is called by that name he is a Northern wizard, white-bearded and wearing a hat like that worn by Odin. When he is called Mithrandir he is different—more Elvish and thus more Welsh. And when he is called Olórin he is different again (though that is only once in *The Lord of the Rings*), being by that name an angelic being, part of quite a different kind of mythology. In short, the use of Old English, Welsh, or Norse necessarily gives an Old English or Welsh or Norse character to the peoples involved. This is, however, only one answer, or one part of the answer: it explains the appeal of the world-in-translation (so to speak), but it does not justify it.

The other—or justifying—part of the answer has to do, I believe, with the fact that languages behave in the same ways, whatever the language, whatever the time—and with one other point. From the root languages (not merely one root language), dialects develop, and these become separate languages (given sufficient time). The ancient unities of archaic languages break down, and the languages simplify (and at the same time become more abstract, or at least capable of greater abstraction). Inflections, tenses, numbers—all slough off. There is, in a sense, nothing new under the sun in even a new language. It is thus perfectly within keeping for a philologist, conscious of all this, to use one language in a given state of its development to represent another language at the same state, and to have the connotations of the one carry over quite properly into the other. This is what Tolkien has done, as he himself noted. If we assume that there resides some kind of *genius* in a land—a hardness in the Northern spirit (and a preservation of things), a kind of sanctity perhaps in the West—then we could expect, as languages rise and fall within that land, that the peoples who speak them will be not unlike each other. There will always—under whatever guise and in whatever time—be an England.

This may seem fanciful (though Tolkien's own statement quoted as an epigraph for the foreword to this book suggests that it is not). What is not fanciful at all—what is quite certain—is that as the mythology of *The Silmarillion* underlies the story of *The Lord of the Rings*, so the languages of Tolkien's Middle-earth underlie that mythology. He himself has told us that the mythology was created for the sake of the languages. And here, I believe, it may be we can find our way better if we take a detour into C. S. Lewis's grab-bag novel, *That Hideous Strength* (a novel which, admittedly, Tolkien did not much like). In that book, Lewis speaks of a language where the meaning is truly inherent in each syllable, as the sun is inherent in each waterdrop, "language herself as she first sprung at Maleldil's bidding out of the molten quicksilver of the star called Mercury on Earth but Viritrilbia in Deep Heaven"(1965, 228)—a language of great words that sound like castles. This language, which Lewis calls Old Solar (but Tolkien would not, I think, have agreed on that name), is his version of Tolkien's eldest tongue, and I think it not inappropriate to use Lewis's lines as a key to Tolkien's belief, though here I speak under correction. (The reason Tolkien originally disliked *That Hideous Strength* was precisely Lewis's syncretism—his combination of Tolkien's mythology and that of Charles Williams.)

To see the connection between the sound of a language and the nature of its speakers, one need only contrast the Black Tongue of the inscription on the One Ring—"Ash nazg durbatûlûk, ash nazg gimbatul, ash nazg thrakatûlûk, agh burzum-ishi krimpatul"—with the language of the Elves—"A Elbereth Gilthoniel / silivren penna miriel / O menel aglor elenath." And it is not only sound that is important: syntax is also. To quote Tolkien's own commentary linking language and character (appendix F): "Orcs and Trolls spoke as they would, without love of words or things, and their language was actually more degraded and filthy than I have shown it. I do not suppose that any will wish for a closer rendering, though models are easy to find. Much the same sort of talk can still be heard among the low-minded; dreary and repetitive with hatred and contempt, too long removed from good to retain even verbal vigour, save in the ears of those to whom only the squalid sounds strong." (Note here the phrase "without love of words or things"—a philologist's linking.)

Similarly, the language of the Ents (Onodrim) is "slow, sonorous, agglomerated, repetitive, indeed long-winded; formed of a multiplicity of vowel-shades and distinctions of tone and quantity which even the lore-masters of the Eldar had not attempted to represent in writing." It is like the Ents themselves—thus Pippin speaking of Treebeard's eyes:

> One felt as if there was an enormous well behind them, filled up with ages of memory and long, slow, steady thinking; but their surface was sparkling with the present: like sun shimmering on the outer leaves of

a vast tree, or on the ripples of a very deep lake. I don't know, but it felt as if something that grew in the ground—asleep, you might say or just feeling itself as something between root-tip and leaf-tip, between deep earth and sky—had suddenly waked up, and was considering you with the same slow care it had given to its own inside affairs for endless years. (II, 83)

There are other examples I could adduce. The hardness of the Dwarvish tongue is appropriate to a race working with stone and metal, even as its gutturals bespeak a people working underground. (We should also remark that the true language and names of the Dwarves—of which we hear little—have a Semitic cast.) The shifts in the Elvish tongues—as in the names of the months—show a kind of "domesticizing" tendency at work (*Narvinyé* to *Narwain, Neninié* to *Ninui, Yavannié* to *Ivanneth, Narquelié* to *Narbeleth*) that is at least parallel to—if it does not in fact denote— the "domesticizing" of those Elves that remained in Middle-earth in the First Age. The Sindarin language, like the Grey Elves, is more of the earth, earthy, than the Quenya and the High Elves who speak it. I use the word "domesticizing" advisedly (I hope) to suggest that both the Grey Elves and the Sindarin tongue over the years grew more at home in Middle-earth. Thus, distantly from *adûn*, the West, comes the *Dun*—of *Dunadan*, the Man of the West. But the Numenorean for "man" is *atan* and for "west" is *adûn*, less comfortable sounds. In the Shire, *Baranduin* becomes Brandywine, and the Elvish name is thoroughly domesticized. Follow where you will, in *The Lord of the Rings*, "Languages are the chief distinguishing marks of peoples. . . . let the languages perish, and the peoples perish too, or become different peoples."

All of this is important for understanding Tolkien's version of Middle-earth. But languages not only reflect the nature of the peoples that use them (which we would expect from Tolkien's scholarly work, even if we knew nothing whatever about *The Lord of the Rings*); they are also, in a sense, the mirror of the action. Moreover, there are subsidiary ways in which *The Lord of the Rings* reveals the contours of a philologist's world. Here I am thinking not so much of Tolkien's verses (which are properly alliterative for the "Old English" Rohirrim, rhymed—perhaps over-rhymed—for the rustic Hobbits) as of his word play. By that I mean not only puns (which are in fact few in number and concentrated among the Hobbits), but the rhythmic prose in which Tom Bombadil speaks and the resounding anticlimax incorporated in names such as Peregrin Took or Lobelia Sackville-Baggins.

It is in fact instructive to see how Tolkien played with these names as he revised his work. When I was a member of the University of Wisconsin Tolkien Society, our never-to-be-finished project was a variorum edition of *The Lord of the Rings* (the manuscript being at Marquette, in Milwaukee), the first and only fruits of which were comparisons of the original Hobbit-names with those of the final version, a comparison showing Tolkien's attempts to achieve precisely this effect. And if anyone doubts that this was habitual in Tolkien's own attitude to things, it would be in order to check his verses on Charles Williams (printed in Humphrey Carpenter's *The Inklings*), ending with the reference to Great Charles's Wain.

But let me return for the moment to language as a mirror of action (and I can see how this fits in with our conjectural reconstruction of language at the time of the Chauvet caves). I will begin by calling to your attention the hymn of the eagle that "bore tidings beyond hope from the Lords of the West, crying 'Sing now, ye people of the Tower of Anor / for the Realm of Sauron is ended for ever! and the Dark Tower is thrown down'" (III, 297). That hymn is clearly and unmistakably modeled on the Hebrew psalms, though Tolkien otherwise virtually eschewed the use of any Hebrew models. It is fair, I think, to ask why this particular exception was made, though I will not answer that question just yet.

Some critics have objected to Tolkien's high-flown diction in those portions of the narrative that concern the Elves and the Men of the West, Eldar and Edaín. The fact that *The Silmarillion* has not been as popular as *The Lord of the Rings* may testify to a general sense that elevated diction needs some relief or counterpoint, or it may testify to the vague sense of Biblical pastiche that seems to underlie the critical objections to Tolkien's use of this style at all. The word "Biblical" is, of course, misleading. We tend to think of Elizabethan (or even medieval) prose as Biblical because the King James Version (Authorized Version)—which was archaic in its own day, and thus very nearly medieval—is the only prose of that kind we read now, except perhaps for a few prose passages in Shakespeare and a meditation or two by John Donne.

Yet the style is equally that of Lord Berners or Sir Walter Ralegh—or Malory. Recall Sir Ector's lament for Lancelot: "And now I dare say thou, Sir Lancelot, there thou liest, thou wert never matched of earthly knight's hand." Or recall King Arthur on the day of battle: "'Now tide me death, tide me life,' said the king, . . . at a better avail shall I never have him." Or (going on to Ralegh), recall the conclusion to his *Historie:* "Whom none could advise, thou hast persuaded, what none hath dared, thou hast done; thou hast taken together all the far-stretched pride, vanity, and ambition of man, and covered it over with these two narrow words, *hic jacet.*" Though Ralegh, like the King James Version, echoes the older style, it is Malory (and perhaps Berners) in whom we find Tolkien's model. Tolkien's persistent use of "and" to begin sentences, and especially to begin paragraphs, is strongly reminiscent of Malory. So, likewise, is the general "medievalism" of his tone—indeed, it is this "Malorian" quality to his prose that has in part, I believe, led to the widespread view that *The Lord of the Rings* is a medieval work. When Tolkien is telling of fair knights and ladies (whether of the Eldar or the Edaín), he is using the diction of the most famous English chronicler of the fair knights and ladies of the Table Round.

Critics have also objected to the rusticity—still more to the children's-story atmosphere—of the opening chapters of *The Lord of the Rings,* characteristics that pretty much justify the Inklings' calling it "Tolkien's new *Hobbit.*" To be sure, the style wavers a bit in *The Lord of the Rings,* while it is consistently more childlike (or, pejoratively, childish) in the earlier book. But rustic action, to a philologist, should be told in rustic language, and a childlike narrative would be appropriate for the doings of "the half-grown Hobbits, the hole-dwellers"—those "Hungry as hunters, the Hobbit children / The laughing folk, the little people" (1965; II, 85). When Frodo and Sam sit on the right and left hand of the king, however, they are *i Pheriannath.* Tolkien's use of different style for different stages of the action may not be entirely successful—that is, there may be technical flaws in his execution of the design he has set for himself—but it is important to see that this is what he is trying to do.

And this answers the question I posed a few paragraphs ago. The eagle speaks in the mode of the psalmist because that is the most exalted, most holy mode of speech that Tolkien can use as (borrowing Eliot's term) an objective correlative for his action—that is, calling a style to mind as *object* in order to suggest to the reader events or feelings that go with that object. (In the same fashion, when Aragorn the King Elessar takes Frodo and Sam up and seats them one on his right and one on his left, we catch an echo of Christ and His apostles—presumably intentional.) Throughout *The Lord of the Rings*, the diction matches, or is intended to match, the action. That there are problems with this approach is obvious, and two of them in particular deserve attention here.

One, quite simply, is that we may not see the objective correlative because we are not familiar with the object. We may not read Malory. We may not all of us have read the Psalms. We may not even have read the right children's stories. *The Lord of the Rings* was read aloud (first by Professor Tolkien and then by his son Christopher) to a small group who called themselves—and are still called—the Inklings. They were not (*pace* Charles Moorman or even, recently, Professor Shippey) a special group of "Oxford Christians." But they were mostly men of a common background, much of an age (except for Christopher), generally Tory in persuasion, and either Church of England or Roman Catholic. We, on the other hand—we readers of *The Lord of the Rings*—are not a group with similar backgrounds. We are not all readers of Malory (though perhaps we should be). And we are certainly not all Tories. That Tolkien's voice comes through to us is part of his genius, but our cloud of unknowing does muffle it.

The second problem is that there is, as I have suggested, an air of pastiche to the whole proceeding—not to the use of language as a mirror of character but to the use of language as a mirror to action. C. S. Lewis once observed that Tolkien's world was like a version of *The Wind in the Willows* in which the battle of Toad Hall had suddenly become a serious *heimsökn* and Badger had begun to talk like Njal. Just so. And that transformation may not be to everyone's taste. More to the point here, it cannot be easy to carry off. I never, as a child, considered Kenneth Grahame's chapter on "The Piper at the Gates of Dawn" at all successful. As an adult, I admit I might revise my view, but in any case the shift is artistically dangerous. And if one shift is dangerous, what of many? Not long ago I picked up a paperback edition of some stories by the American regionalist and (if I may use the word) "pastichist," August Derleth. After reading the first few stories, I thought,

"Here is August Derleth being Montague Rhodes James." I
turned to the last two stories, read them, and observed to myself,
"Here is August Derleth being H. P. Lovecraft." But where was he
being August Derleth?

Now Tolkien is certainly being himself in the sub-creation of
The Lord of the Rings: if the work is not absolutely *sui generis*, that
is only because it has bred imitators. But there lurks at the back of
the mind a not-entirely-organized thought that this high diction is
"only" Tolkien being Sir Thomas Malory. We are used to authors
whose styles are self-consistent. Hemingway's style is recognizable
at fifty paces. Milton's style may go flat (as in the "untransmuted
lump of futurity" that concludes *Paradise Lost*), but flat or
rounded, it is clearly his. Wordsworth's style, though easy to par-
ody, can with difficulty be confused with anyone else's. Charles
Williams wrote a prose which is virtually inimitable (fortunately so,
in the view of some critics—but see, recently, my edition of his
Detective Fiction Reviews 1930–1935). But what is it we are speaking of when we speak of Tolkien's style? The idea of *The Lord of
the Rings*, the story, the peoples, the view of mythology, the whole
sub-creation—these are recognizably his. The style seems to be
another matter. Deliberately so.

At the risk of falling straight into the intentional fallacy I would
argue that the shifts in style are part of the philologist's world of
The Lord of the Rings and that the approach has perfectly
respectable antecedents. Not surprisingly, the one that comes first
to mind is medieval, indeed quintessentially medieval. You will
recall the Reeve's Tale in *The Canterbury Tales*, the northern 'rim,
ram, ruf, by lettre." You may also recall that the classic study of
Chaucer as philologist (in the Reeve's Tale) is by Tolkien. But the
Reeve's Tale is only one example of Chaucer's shifting style (compare *Sir Thopas*, the Knight's Tale, the Wife of Bath's Tale) and his
use of language as a key to character. Of course, in *The Canterbury
Tales*, the action—that is, the tale told—itself reflects the character
of the teller. Tolkien, on the other hand, orchestrates a vast polyphonic narrative, a feigned history told mostly by one teller. He
cannot shift narrators, and he cannot shift tales, because it is all one
tale (though, to be sure, the past is filled in by Elrond and others).
One could, I suppose, speak of *The Lord of the Rings* as an amal-
gam of Chaucer and Malory, but others beside Chaucer have fitted
style to action (*Beowulf*, for example), and, on the other hand,

Tolkien's whole complex endeavor is really something that has not been tried before.

I am no musician, but it has struck me that music provides an analogy for this use of style to represent action. That, in itself, says nothing of Tolkien's success. Beethoven used familiar themes to represent the English ("Rule Britannia") and the French ("Malbrouck"), and rifle fire to represent rifle fire, in what some have considered one of the most thoroughly atrocious pieces of music known to man. But if we think of words as Tolkien's notes, and the arrangement of words as a form of musical composition, we will at least be looking at *The Lord of the Rings* as a thing made, and its author as a maker, a poet in the Greek sense of the word. I said that what Tolkien essayed had not been done before, and now I seem to be saying that, in one way or another, it has been. All I am in fact doing is seeking analogies to explain this philologist's view of words and language and how it is given form and life in *The Lord of the Rings.* Things like this have been done before, yes, but not quite like this. (I would note, by the way, that this approach through music finds support in Humphrey Carpenter's view that young Ronald's lack of interest in the piano might be traced to the fact that "words took the place of music for him.")

It is now time to return to the other part of the philologist's view of language, the connection between words and things. In one sense, of course, the connection is that some words— nouns—are the names of things. Indeed, "noun" and "name" are both from *nomen.* But this, though true, is only the beginning of the story. The Orcs, we recall, spoke without love of words or things, and we have already noted how this mode of speaking reveals the Orkish character. Tolkien's description of it does more: besides recalling this words-and-things approach to philology, it at least hints at a normative view of the linguistic process. It seems to be saying that those who love a thing will, and should, seek to enshrine it in beautiful words. Gimli, struck with the beauty of Galadriel, sought a single hair of her head, to be enshrined in imperishable crystal as an heirloom of his house: the skill of the Dwarves was in their hands, not in their tongues, or so it was said. But in the same wise, if we have any skill with words, we should seek to match beauty with beauty. Nouns must not only describe things, but suggest them, in a kind of onomatopoiesis. A noun is the name of a thing, as the old grammar books have it, but the question before us is one not so much of grammar as of gramarye.

For the plain fact and the rest of the story is that words, and especially names, are magic. It is fitting and proper that the gates of Moria should open to a magic word. It is fitting and proper that in the very depths of the earth, the deepest evil of all (deeper than Sauron, deeper even than the Balrogs) is nameless (II, 134) and that Gandalf, returned thence, will not speak of it. It is fitting and proper (and a related point) that the enemies of Mordor will not mention the name of Mordor, and that a rebuke follows a light-hearted Hobbit reference to Frodo as the Lord of the Rings.

I am reminded of an old joke about Adam and Eve on naming day in Eden. Eve suggests to Adam that a particular beast be called a rhinoceros, and when asked why, responds, "It looks more like a rhinoceros than anything we've seen yet." The joke is, if funny, anti-Platonic: that is, it assumes there is no pre-existing idea of *rhinoceros* to which the beast in question can be compared. But if there is a "proper" name—a "real" name—for every beast, then to know that name is to know the beast, and, more important here, to speak that name, as our books of lore tell us, is to control the beast. Nor does this hold only for beasts. When Treebeard cautions the Hobbits about their hastily revealing their real names, what they call themselves; when it is recounted that the Dwarves reveal their true names to no one; when Gandalf, on his return, says that Legolas and Gimli and Aragorn "may still call me Gandalf"—we are at the edges of the realm where names are magic. If your enemy knows your name, he may command you. In the nineteenth century, when an African king died, his name passed out of the language, lest it be spoken thereafter and the speaker command the king's spirit. And the vowel-less Name of God, the Tetragrammaton, could be pronounced only by the High Priest in the Holy of Holies on the Day of Atonement. We are not far from this naming magic.

Like other children of the eighteenth century, the science of philology reached its period of greatest achievement (and greatest excitement) around the end of the nineteenth. The New English Dictionary was and is a measure of that achievement, but there are others. There was a sudden interest in African and other exotic languages, marked by the publication of classic studies of tongues in the Rhodesian and Nigerian areas, ethnolinguistic research in

Papua, studies of Amerindian speech, the rebirth (however artificial) of the Welsh and Irish languages. Certainly one of the things that gave impetus to philological study was the discovery of new languages in hitherto unexplored areas. (It has occurred to me that Rider Haggard's interest in Africa—and Haggard did profoundly influence Tolkien—included an interest in its languages, but my friend, Professor Norman Etherington, thinks I may be exaggerating this.)

It might be said that, just as the Edwardian adventure story had its roots in the great explorations of the nineteenth century, so in part did the philological impulse. A generation of scholars—of whom Tolkien was one of the last—was caught in a web of words that stretched from India (where, in effect, it began with the researches of Sir William Jones) all the way around the world to the South Pacific. This web stretched, and stretches, both in time and space. It is a long tale, and not unlike the tale of the years of Middle-earth:

> "But that's a long tale, of course, and goes on past the happiness and into grief and beyond it—and the Silmaril went on and came to Eärendil. And why sir, I never thought of that before! We've got—you've got some of the light of it in that star-glass that the Lady gave you! Why, to think of it, we're in the same tale still! It's going on. Don't the great tales never end?"

> "No, they never end as tales," said Frodo (II, 408).

I said in the last chapter that the difference between the brief (even slapdash) creation of such books as *King Solomon's Mines* or *The Lost World* and the long slow growth of *The Lord of the Rings* was in part attributable to the influence of Tolkien's professional life. In part it is the difference between a scholar's sub-creation and that of a professional writer, by which I mean one making a living from his writing. But it is also the difference between a writer accustomed to following words and languages over the sweep of centuries and continents, and one not so accustomed. This is not to say that Haggard, in particular, does not from time to time feel the fascination of languages: it was, after all, the Shard of Amyntas in *She* that may have helped set Professor Tolkien on the road to his life's work. But only Tolkien wrote an Edwardian adventure story with the sweep of the philologist's world.

I had originally thought of approaching Tolkien's Middle-earth through its specifically medieval characteristics—writing of the "medievalist's world" of *The Lord of the Rings*—and certainly that would not be a difficult approach to take. But this approach through "medievalism" has been taken in the past, and the results have not been especially encouraging. Moreover, C. S. Lewis was a medievalist, but for all his close friendship with Tolkien, the world of his novels is not much like the world of Tolkien's, except where he is borrowing from Tolkien's world. When one contrasts the hit-or-miss eclecticism of the Narnia stories (especially *The Lion, the Witch, and the Wardrobe*) with Tolkien's careful use of linguistic objective correlatives, one can see just how much difference Tolkien's philology made. For Lewis, though a medievalist, and though in some ways a student of words (even author of a book, *Studies on Words*—which, however, Tolkien did not like), was not a philologist and did not think or write like one. Tolkien did.

Lewis, instead, writes in pictures. Indeed, most of his books begin with pictures, and his approach is essentially visual (he even wrote a short essay on his writing procedure, "It All Began With A Picture"). Tolkien's approach is not. One can draw pictures from his words, but the pictures are one's own, not his. That is, of course, part of the use of language as a correlative for action, which is one of the four ways in which the world of *The Lord of the Rings* is a philologist's world.

Let me give some examples of this "nonpictorial" nature of *The Lord of the Rings*. A notable passage is Tolkien's description of Théoden riding forth to battle: "With that he seized a great horn from Guthláf his banner-bearer, and he blew such a blast upon it that it burst asunder. And straightway all the horns in the host were lifted up in music, and the blowing of the horns of Rohan in that hour was like a storm upon the plain and a thunder in the mountains" (III, 137–38).

A few lines later comes what is ostensibly visual description: "His golden shield was uncovered, and lo! it shone like an image of the Sun, and the grass flamed into green about the white feet of his steed. For morning came, morning and a wind from the sea." Here we have colors, but we create the picture from those colors; it is not created for us. Similarly, the description of Aragorn's coming in with the captured fleet is almost entirely auditory: "Thus came Aragorn son of Arathorn, Elessar, Isildur's heir, out of the

Paths of the Dead, borne upon a wind from the Sea to the kingdom of Gondor; and the mirth of the Rohirrim was a torrent of
laughter and a flashing of swords, and the joy and wonder of the
City was a music of trumpets and a ringing of bells" (III, 150).

And, a few paragraphs later, there is a passage that at first seems
to be visual description, but is not really so: "Then the Sun went
at last behind Mindolluin and filled all the sky with a great burning, so that the hills and the mountains were dyed as with blood;
fire glowed in the River, and the grass of the Pelennor lay red in
the nightfall." Here, once more, we have colors—or rather, one
color—but it is the words and the connotations they bear (and the
echoes of other words, dimly blowing in the hills) out of which we
construct the picture.

Not only do the auditory images precede the visual, but the
visual images are of a particular and unusual kind. Tolkien is not
always describing so much as "connoting." It is the approach of an
author peculiarly conscious of words as words. It is also an
approach that virtually precludes the description of anything outside the reader's experience (whether actual or Jungian), which
means that Middle-earth in the Third Age cannot be much different from Middle-earth in the second millennium AD. For otherwise, what is the significance (or *significans*) of the words?

I have already suggested that a philologist would find it appropriate, given the universal nature of the laws of language, to use
the language of one age and people to represent that of another
age and people (assuming some similarity of nature), and that he
might find it particularly appropriate if it is a people of the same
part of Middle-earth. One of the themes of Tolkien's work is the
Englishness of England: that is at the root of *Farmer Giles of Ham*,
with its story of Aegidius de Hammo and Chrysophylax Dives,
anglicé Farmer Giles and the Dragon. This theme of Englishness is
combined with an un-English kind of art. It has been argued that
the Englishness of English art resides in the view that the purpose
of art is to preach, and the best preaching comes in accurately
observing the detailed minutiae of daily life. In this sense, Chaucer
is English, Malory is English (I recall that C. S. Lewis gave us some
examples of this), C. S. Lewis (though Irish) is English, but
Tolkien, like Rudyard Kipling, is not. Perhaps that has something
to do with the fact that he, like Kipling, was enamored of
"Englishry." Or perhaps it was because he studied the English lan-

guage, partly from the outside, thus seeing it clearly and with the same clear vision saw the beauty of Englishry. (The business of using a language of one people to represent the language of another people at the same stage has a slight Spenglerian sound to it, but it is slight enough, I think, not to be taken amiss.)

To some extent, as I have suggested, C. S. Lewis can be used as a key to understanding Tolkien, and particularly Lewis's so-called space trilogy, inasmuch as that was written during the time of Tolkien's maximum influence on Lewis. I would be confident in using *Out of the Silent Planet* or *Perelandra* in this way (though they are in fact not particularly useful for the purpose), but of *That Hideous Strength* I am not so sure. The Ransom of the first two books, who is, like Tolkien, a philologist, becomes in the third book a kind of Charles Williams, and the mythology grows Williams-ish as well (even though it contains references to Númenor). I cannot be sure that Lewis's views here are (if either) from Williams or from Tolkien—which is unfortunate, because one or two passages indicate a belief in an English genius, resident in the land.

After some consideration, I believe this comes in, originally, from William Blake, through Owen Barfield, and thus belongs to Tolkien through Lewis—but it *does* belong to Tolkien, not Williams. In any case, such a belief would provide a philosophical basis for Tolkien's doctrine of translation. And it would help round off our explanation of the paradox whereby what is avowedly a translation of a feigned distant past into a recognizable England (something like what Professor Shippey calls a "calque" in his *The Road to Middle-earth*) attracts us precisely by its Englishry. We might note that this implies separated development of languages rather than diffusion from one original language—which, of course, is what we came up with earlier in this chapter.

All this is not to say that *The Lord of the Rings* preaches a particular philological doctrine—at least, not beyond *wörter und sächer*. Tolkien is no Lévi-Strauss; he is not concerned with relating the structure of language to the structure of thought (or of being). No more is he a Dumézil exploring the structure of religion. And just as it is important to realize that philology does not explain Tolkien's achievement (however much it explains his technique), so it is important to realize what Tolkien is not doing and is not trying to do. Because his Middle-earth is a philologist's world, there are several things it is not. Because he was a particular kind of philologist, there are several other things it is not.

Because words are used in the way they are, they cannot be used for pure description. I know from my own experience with the book that the connotations and linguistic objective correlatives tend to outweigh the actual description. It was not until somewhere around the umpteenth rereading that I formed an accurate picture of the abode of the Elves in Lothlórien. I am not sure how well I could set out the seven circles of Minas Tirith. I could describe Bag End, but what I would be describing, I think, is Badger's house in *The Wind in the Willows.* Could one recognize Minas Tirith without the names, and outside *The Lord of the Rings?* Perhaps. Perhaps we should find out a way to find out. But in the meantime, we can say, in short, that the philologist's world of *The Lord of the Rings* is not a miniaturist's world or a world where we read the details of the story of daily life—and in that restricted sense, not an example of the Englishness of English Art (on which see Nikolaus Pevsner's *The Englishness of English Art* and my forthcoming *The Rise of Tolkienian Fantasy*).

It is not a structural anthropologist's world, either: Tolkien was emphatically not Lévi-Strauss. I do not claim to understand everything Lévi-Strauss says, but it is clear that to him the relationship of words (sentence and syntagm) is more important than the words themselves. Words in language, like things in economic transactions, are counters in a set of (chiefly triangular) relationships. The structure, not the words, is the message. Now it is true that Tolkien was not uninterested in language structure (the language of the Ents, in particular, shows that), but it is equally true that the anthropological approach to literature was largely anathema to him. Indeed, when Lewis was asked to contribute an essay to the *festschrift* for Tolkien's seventieth birthday, he responded with an attack on the anthropological approach, ending with the words: "The forest is, after all, enchanted: the mares have built nests in every tree." In short, *The Lord of the Rings* is not a work whose world is to be approached through structural anthropology—or, indeed, through any form of structuralism.

In a way, this lack of interest in structure (even in this peculiar sense) may seem curious in a world where relationships are of paramount importance, and still more curious when that world is the sub-creation of a man particularly interested in words and language. But there are relationships and relationships—those that are irreducible or mathematical, and those that are personal or cultural. With the first of these, *The Lord of the Rings* is not much concerned: it is the relationship of master and man, of liege and liege-lord, of companions in adversity ("we few, we happy few"), of king and high-king—the personal and cultural relationships— that are the stuff of Western culture and of Tolkien's Middle-earth. We look not for new vision, new explanation of the way things are, but for ancient verities. For philology, in Tolkien's practice, is historical—the past, as I have said, alive in the present.

To be conscious of the past alive in the present, one must of course be conscious that the past is different from the present; otherwise there would be neither mystery nor excitement in its survival. (That this is a gift of Walter Scott, and, for Tolkien, of Fenimore Cooper coming from Scott, ties this with chapter 1.) The structuralist looks at what is constant, the historian at what changes or has changed. In his feigned history of *The Lord of the Rings* Tolkien is concerned with both historical minutiae and with the sweep of history and because this is so, we respond to his world in a particular fashion. To a structuralist we might say, "Ah, yes, now I see the underlying patterns—now the way things work is made plain." But for Tolkien our response is, "Yes, this is how Hobbits ought to speak, and how proud, brave, beautiful princes and kings must have spoken and acted in the great and romantic times of long ago." And our disbelief is suspended, and the long ago becomes part of our now.

You will recall, once again, Tolkien's reaction to the story of the juniper tree in Grimm, his perception of distance and a great abyss of time not measurable even by twe tusend Jöhr. We have come more or less full circle in our discussion of the philologist's world of *The Lord of the Rings*, back to the past alive in the present, and especially in language. (And, once again, with Cooper, as with the Grimms collecting their tales, in the forests.) I would suggest that it is not coincidental that the same brothers Grimm who collected the fairy tales were philologists—in fact, among the first philologists. I would suggest that Tolkien is their disciple in both respects. And I would suggest, finally that those who see in him the teller of tales, though they are certainly right in what they see, are seeing something less than the whole truth. Tolkien's half-century of working life as a philologist caught him firmly in that web of words that is always and everywhere interwoven in his imaginative work; without that web *The Lord of the Rings* would be very different—indeed, it probably would not be at all.

3

The Timeless Moment in *The Lord of the Rings*: Christian Doctrine in a Pre-Christian Age

God is the Lord of angels,
and of men—and of elves.
Legend and History have met and fused.

—J. R. R. TOLKIEN, "On Fairy-Stories"

Now God be thanked, Who has matched us with this hour,
And caught our youth, and wakened us from sleeping.

—RUPERT BROOKE, "1914. I. Peace"

When *The Silmarillion* was finally published in 1977, it made perfectly clear what had been seen in a glass darkly (perhaps more darkly than needed be) in *The Lord of the Rings*: Tolkien's Middle-earth is part of a Christian universe (though one in which Christ has not yet come). This seems to contrast rather oddly with the sometimes-heard (or -read) assertion—in the quarter-century from the first publication of *The Lord of the Rings*—that Tolkien's world was a world without concern for the gods. I think I first came across that assertion in Linwood Carter's *Tolkien: A Look Behind The Lord of the Rings*, where Tolkien is compared unfavorably with Lord Dunsany in this respect. But let us consider what a Christian universe before Christ's coming must be. After all, the eighteenth Baron Dunsany might wear his ancient religion lightly in the light-hearted tales whose greatest creation was the unfortunate king whom the gods decreed must not only cease to be but cease ever to have been. But John Ronald Reuel Tolkien—orphan, convert, Catholic schoolboy, emigrant—did not wear his religion lightly. As his biographer has stated, he wanted his stories "to express his own moral view of the universe, and as a Christian he could not place this view in a cosmos without the God that he worshipped" (Carpenter 1977, 103).

A Christian world in pre-Christian times must still be a world nurtured by the Christian God. Certainly there might be those who worshipped false gods. There might be fallen gods, true powers but demonic (like Lucifer and his legions). And there might be, as in our own world, in pagan times, true gods or images of true gods worshipped falsely. It happens that, in *The Silmarillion*, we learn something about fallen powers and about their history, but we learn virtually nothing of this in *The Lord of the Rings*—though certainly we know Morgoth and Sauron to be not only evil but fallen powers, if by instinct (and by the fact that Sauron was one fair to look upon). Of the false or partly false worship of the gods, Tolkien had much to say in life (especially in the conversation that brought about C. S. Lewis's conversion), but little here.

Of course, in *The Lord of the Rings* there are angels (*angeloi*, messengers), but they are far from being gods. We know the angelic name of one of these beings—Olórin—but he does not act like a Christian angel, at least as we in these days understand them to act. In any case, the reason for keeping the gods out of *The Lord of the Rings* may be the inability to accommodate something like polytheism to a universe of moral absolutes. Or the reason may be artistic. Each referent-language—Welsh for Elves, Norse for Dwarves—has its own attached pantheon, and a multiplication of pantheons would be distracting. Whatever the immediate reasons, Tolkien has done what, as a Catholic, he should have been expected to do: he has created a monotheistic universe.

It is true that, in *The Silmarillion*, there is a system (a pantheon, if you will) set out along the lines Lewis imagined in his Ransom stories—which are the lines Tolkien had set out in that famous conversation with Lewis and Dyson seventy years ago that led toward Lewis's reconversion. But in *The Lord of the Rings* there is only fleeting reference to God ("the One" in III, 392) and to the gods ("Valar"). The reasons for this are essentially theological. Just as the ancient Athenians could erect an altar to the Unknown God, but could not know Him until St. Paul came to preach Him, so also the ancient peoples of Tolkien's Middle-earth could not know Him without the preaching. And the preaching comes (as it must come) with Christ.

The word *preaching* reminds me that there is one obvious respect in which Tolkien's world—as a philologist's creation— must fit into the Christian view. The great prologue to the *Gospel* of St. John tells us that "In the beginning was the *Word*." Whether, as with Tolkien in *The Silmarillion* (or Lewis, derivatively, in *The Magician's Nephew*), it is the sung Word or the spoken, in the end is of little importance, so long as (and it is true, even, implicitly, in *Genesis*) creation is in fact a kind of utterance. I think, also, in *The Lord of the Rings*, there is a kind of Sacrament of the Word, as when Aragorn claims his kingdom, "Out of the Great Sea to Middle-earth I am come. In this place will I abide, and my heirs, unto the ending of the world" (III, 303)—"*Et Eärello Endorenna utúlien. Sinome maruvan ar Hildinyar tenn' Ambar-metta!*" (I am told that the Sacrament of the Word was counted as one of the sacraments in our world up to the time of Hugh of St. Victor in the twelfth century: this is clearly a sacramental use, by Aragorn, in his coronation, of the words of Elendil, "when he came up out of the sea on the wings of the wind.")

Here I should take what may seem a slight detour. One of the unexamined questions about the moral world of *The Lord of the Rings* is the presence of the apparently wholly good (Aragorn, perhaps Faramir, perhaps even Éomer) in what we assume to be a fallen world. One senses a hierarchy of good, or a saving (and unfallen) remnant, or both. Once again, I would turn to C. S. Lewis for enlightenment. In *Perelandra*, the King asks Ransom if he does not remember that in the first generations after the Fall, the people were long livers (to which Ransom responds that most men take that for a story or a poetry). The long lives of the first kings of Númenor (from Elros Tar-Minyatur), though explained by what seems a different *machina ex Deo*, are likewise reminiscences of a paradise lately lost—but not, witness Aragorn, and this is my point, entirely lost. I am not, of course, suggesting that Lewis influenced Tolkien—quite the contrary ("No one ever influenced Tolkien—you might as well try to influence a Bandersnatch!"). But this picture was in both their minds at the time, in the great days of the Inklings—though, doubtless, in Lewis's mind because in Tolkien's. Be that as it may, the reason I bring this up is to suggest the presence, in Tolkien's Middle-earth, of divine powers and reminiscences of divinity—and perhaps more than reminiscences. "A faint breath, as Vergil says, reaches even the late generations" (Lewis 1990, 201). The point deserves elaboration.

We are not dealing here with a Sprague de Camp sort of world where the laws of magic replace the laws of science. We are dealing with our own world, in a feigned past to be sure, but one in which the same physical laws hold as hold in our time—and the same spiritual and moral laws. "Good and ill have not changed since yesteryear; nor are they one thing among Elves and Dwarves and another among Men. It is a man's part to discern them, as much in the Golden Wood as in his own house" (II, 50). Recall the First Epistle to the Corinthians (12:7–11), recounting the ninefold gifts of the Holy Spirit: the word of wisdom, the word of knowledge, faith, gifts of healing, the working of miracles, prophecy discerning of spirits, divers kinds of tongues (that is, speaking in tongues), and interpretation of tongues. It is the word "discern" that led me to the passage in St. Paul, but the whole catalogue of gifts seems to me highly relevant. For consider.

Wisdom and knowledge inhere in the Elves, the Wizards, and the Men of the West (perhaps also in the Dwarves, though they seem, in a Christian cosmogony, to be dwellers in Limbo, missing the Spirit—or, as our world has it, in our medieval Catholic doctrine, the virtuous Pagans or Jews to be saved from Limbo by Christ in the Harrowing of Hell). In Aragorn are the gifts of healing; in Gandalf the working of miracles; in Saruman and in the Mirror of Galadriel the gift of prophecy; in all the Nine Walkers except Boromir (and in Faramir, Éomer, Théoden) faith, in some discernment; and in the whole creation the gifts of tongues and the interpretation of tongues. It may be noted here, also, that Aragorn may be taken as a Christ figure to the extent that in him the ancient Adamite unity of Prophet, Priest, and King seems to hold, as it holds in the new creation in Christ, before being separated again in His successors in our world—Peter, James, and John. But this may be thought tendentious. What is important here is that the gifts of the Spirit are present, and the Spirit thus abroad, in Tolkien's Middle-earth.

This is true despite the fact that no reference is made to the Spirit, and only the one passing reference to God. And the lack of such reference is exactly what we should expect. If we understand—with those churches that accept the *filioque*—that the Holy Spirit proceeds from the Father and the Son, "neither made nor created nor begotten but proceeding," then we must see that a theology consistent with this doctrine cannot define the Spirit without knowing the Son. By definition, in a pre-Christian age, Christ the Son cannot be known, and neither therefore can the Holy Spirit. At the same time, reference to the Father (in that Person) would be inaccurate—or at the very least is only partially understandable—without reference to the other Persons of the Trinity. But not fatally inaccurate, because this is a pre-Christian age in a *Christian* world.

The claim has, of course, been made that Tolkien's world is non-Christian rather than pre-Christian—that he has taken the world of the Norse gods (or their English analogues) pretty much pure and undiluted. This claim sometimes takes the form of arguing that the world of *The Lord of the Rings* is essentially the world of *Beowulf*, overlooking the fact that the world of *Beowulf* is itself no longer Pagan. But whatever form it takes, there is a certain power to the argument, and I would like to deal with it briefly. The essential point made in this argument is that Tolkien's Middle-earth has no Christian "feel" to it. Because, I believe, the analogue languages have no Christian "feel" to them. The languages that he uses as objective correlatives do carry suggestions of the gods acknowledged by those who used the languages. Gandalf in his hat does indeed recall Odin. So far the point is valid. But we are speaking of theology rather than religion, and the theology of *The Lord of the Rings* is uncompromisingly Christian and Catholic.

In what relation, then, do the Nine Walkers stand to God and to His servants? First, as we have noted, Gandalf is an angel, a messenger of the Valar. Second, Aragorn is one of the Men of the West, long-lived, of Elven descent, in a position analogous perhaps to that of the early Hebrew patriarchs, except that "being . . . of the blood of the West unmingled" he is (being good) purely good, not mixed. Third, Legolas, being one of the Firstborn, is in—or, certainly, capable of—a more direct communication with divinity than is possible for humankind (just how much more direct I do not know). Fourth, Gimli is apart, bound to Middle-earth, until "saved" by his love for the Lady Galadriel. (Some have seen in this an analogue to the salvation of the Jews by the intercession of the

Virgin.) And here we should pause to consider what is "middle" about Middle-earth.

Heaven and Hell, according to the medieval English lyric, are eating into merry Middle-earth—Heaven from above, Hell from below. Middle-earth is not permanent in its present incarnation, neither in Tolkien's world nor in ours. We can expect, some day, a new heaven and a new earth, and in Tolkien's world, consider the conversation of Treebeard with Celeborn and Galadriel (III, 320–21): "It is long, long since we met by stock or by stone, *A vanimai vanimalion nostari!*" he said. "It is sad that we should meet only thus at the ending. For the world is changing: I feel it in the water, I feel it in the earth, and I smell it in the air. I do not think we shall meet again."

And Celeborn said: "I do not know, Eldest." But Galadriel said: "Not in Middle-earth, nor until the lands that lie under the wave are lifted up again. Then in the willow-meads of Tasarinan we may meet in the Spring. Farewell!" Note here the word "nor." The meeting is not to take place in Middle-earth, *and* it is not to take place until Númenor is raised up. In a three-tiered universe, Númenor would be part of Middle-earth, as would any Isles of the Blest. But apparently it is not part of Tolkien's Middle-earth.

In fact, Tolkien's Middle-earth is not three-tiered so much as three-directional. If the West is Heaven (or Paradise), then the East in some sense approaches Hell, even though the symmetry is incomplete, and Middle-earth is middle because betwixt West and East. This reading fits in with the land under the wave and Middle-earth as separate entities: by it, the Undying Lands remain forever beyond the circles of the world, reachable only by the Old Straight Track. By it, Númenor (or, rather, the Isle of Elenna) will be raised up, the world—Middle-earth included—will be changed, and the dead will be raised (III, 428). The distinction between Elenna and Middle-earth holds (III, 303, 390), and we may provisionally accept the view that Tolkien has shifted the "middleness" from a three-tiered to a three-directional universe.

There are, however, tiers within the universe—or, if one prefers, hierarchies. Or, at least, there is a principle of hierarchy. As Professor Scheps has pointed out (1975, 49), the uses of power in *The Lord of the Rings* are strictly defined according to a rigid hierarchy, and one clear distinction between the forces of good and the forces of evil is that the forces of good abide by the restrictions imposed by their place in the hierarchy and the forces of evil (being in rebellion) do not. Professor Scheps called this a "Fairy-tale" morality. I suppose that may be true—after all, our fairy tales (many of them) took their present shape in medieval Christendom's last centuries, Milton's full telling of the rebellion of the forces of evil took shape just after, and this order by hierarchy fits with the hierarchies of medieval Christendom. Of which Shakespeare wrote, "Take but degree away, untune that string / And hark! What discord follows!" Or, as Professor Scheps remarks, "There are indeed greater and lesser men in Middle-earth, and their responsibilities and powers must be used according to the place of each in the natural hierarchy, if that hierarchy, and indeed Middle-earth itself, are to survive" (49–50).

We are thus confronted with a theological question: is a hierarchical ordering of the world (which we clearly have) an indication that we are in a Christian universe? Certainly the Hosts of Heaven, the Nine Orders of the Heavenly Host (of Charles Williams's favorite Pseudo-Dionysius), the *panthea* of earlier Heavens (including that of the *Enuma Elish*), all this hierarchy and its tradition are part of our Christian universe. At the very least, we *may* here be in a Christian world, in a pre-Christian age. There is nothing incompatible with that. Now, with our three-directioned universe, we are confronted with another theological question. If we put Tolkien's Uttermost West and all his West-Middle-East cosmogony into the same figurative category as the three-tiered universe and its cosmogonies, with the same kind of mythological truth, can we reconcile the truths behind (or within) the two? The myths—the cosmogonies—are different, but the truth should be the same. To determine whether it is, we should continue the tale of the Nine Walkers. (We may also attempt a kind of Lewisian syncretism to see how these truths might be reconciled—but not just now.)

Since the prevalence of the Hobbits is what chiefly distinguishes *The Lord of the Rings* from other tales of what used to be called derring-do, and also what (I believe) has determined its popularity, we should expect to find in the relationship of the Hobbits to divinity something of importance to the theological world of *The Lord of the Rings*, and so, in a sense, we do. The thing of importance is that the Hobbits have, at the outset of the story, no connection with divinity beyond what has been handed on (languages, a few proverbs) from men and, ultimately from the Men of the West. This would approximate a normal mortal condition, assuming Christian theology in a pre-Christian age—with one qualification.

Aragorn, as we have seen, is unfallen, and Legolas also. Evil had entered into the world long before, in the person of Morgoth, but I can find no trace of original sin in any of the Nine Walkers, even (though this is a borderline case) in Boromir. Temptation there is, to be sure, as with Boromir, and Pippin (with the *palantir*), and Frodo (at the Crack of Doom); and temptation can be yielded to, as with Gollum and, indeed, Frodo, and Boromir. There is jealousy between Elf and Dwarf, a certain stiffness of neck and loving of company in misery, but there is no universal predisposition to evil. In that sense we are in an age older than Eden, a prelapsarian state in which angelic beings (even, C. S. Lewis would say, the "gods") are striving for humankind (and Hobbitkind). It thus becomes increasingly difficult to fit Tolkien's feigned history into our own (real, feigned, or mythic), unless of course we alter the story of Adam and Eve, or subsume *The Lord of the Rings* within that story.

The Hobbits might seem thus to be without original sin as they are without God. By our own standards, their theological status would be very odd—as odd as the idea of a yet unfallen world, upon which, indeed, that theological status is based. It is here that those who have objected to the absence of religion in *The Lord of the Rings* have put a finger on something of importance, though the objections seem to me to involve some misunderstanding. The progress of the Hobbits—Frodo, Sam, Merry, and Pippin—among the Nine Walkers can be seen as a progress toward spiritual awareness, toward the gift of knowledge if you will, indeed toward the gifts of the Holy Spirit generally. (I wonder if there is a folkloric analogue in the entry of a full human soul into a leprechaun with baptism?)

I might mention here Frodo's treatment of Saruman (wisdom) and understanding of what he is (discernment), as well as his foretelling Sam's children (prophecy); I might mention Sam's own gardening—in part with Galadriel's help—and especially the mallorn tree (miracles), as well as the general increase in faith and knowledge. Sam also has the gift of prophecy in his knowledge that "he had something to do before the end"—though the gift here is inchoate. And he and Frodo have something of a gift in languages—indeed, the knowledge of Elvish confers a kind of special status within the Hobbit world.

We can say then, that although religion as we usually understand that word is absent in the Hobbits, surely the workings of the Spirit are there, more and more as time and the story go on. That the first state, in our own Middle-earth, is rarer even than the second (which is certainly rare), does not alter the fact that the state is presumably characteristic not only of the Hobbits but of others in *The Lord of the Rings* as well. The pilgrim's progress of Meriadoc and Peregrin is evidence of this—and Gandalf the Grey is both angel and pilgrim. (But let us be very clear that I am not saying, in a kind of twenty-first century slogan, that "this is a spiritual book, but not a religious one." That would, in this case, merely be playing with words.)

The workings of the Spirit are not characteristically to be observed in Boromir, the last of our walkers. Indeed, Boromir, of all the characters in the book, is most like us: a human mixture of good and evil impulses. One could construct a critical system based on that fact, making Boromir the "hero" of *The Lord of the Rings*—a system not unlike that which, on similar grounds, makes Satan the "hero" of *Paradise Lost*—were it not that Boromir (fortunately, were we to try this) disappears from the action early in the story. It remains true, whatever our critical system, that the blood of the Númenoreans does not run true in Boromir: he is, in essence, a mere man, and though his story is *germane* to our purposes and to *The Lord of the Rings*, he is in fact *necessary* only to Denethor and Denethor's story—it being Boromir's story, in fact, that is the proximate cause of Denethor's downfall.

Though this "mere manhood" of Boromir represents a problem in literary criticism (since the Hobbits are the "mere men" through whom the action of *The Lord of the Rings* is mediated and recorded), it is not a theological stumbling block. Boromir is one of the "nations" rather than one of the "people"—the gentile, the *goy*, the outsider (though, properly, these terms should, of course, apply to Dwarves and non-Dwarves, since they are the Jews of Tolkien's calque on England—on which see or rather hear his BBC interview with Denis Guérolt). Boromir falls, but recovers: yet though he recovers, he is clearly (from the very beginning) a lesser man than the others. To be sure, Númenoreans can fall: Denethor does, in whom the blood runs "nearly true," and back in history

(as appendix A tells us) Ar-Pharazôn the Golden broke the Ban of
the Valar and set foot upon the Undying Lands, a fall greater than
Denethor's. Yet there is a greatness in Ar-Pharazôn and his followers, even in Denethor, beyond (I think) the greatness in
Boromir—they would be greater in good or in evil (though, of
course, Boromir repented, and they did not).

What this portends, I believe, is not merely a hierarchical ordering of the sorts and conditions of men, not merely a celebration of
a saving remnant, not even that *corruptio optimi pessima* ("the
higher they are, the further they fall"), but a view that Christ and
only Christ is the great leveler. (That point is made also in Lewis's
That Hideous Strength, in the discussion of Christmas.) In our Old
Testament, though the chosen people can be aided by the *goyim*
(Cyrus, King of Persia, being the obvious example), the chosen—
the "people"—remain the chosen, and the gentiles—the
"nations"—remain the gentiles. It is only in the New Testament,
and especially in St. Paul, that the nations can be taken into the
Kingdom. Similarly in Tolkien's pre-Christian age, there is a distinction between the Men of the West and lesser men, and the
Christ has not come to bridge the gap. Presumably salvation exists
for these "lesser breeds" so long as they are not without the law,
nor will it be a salvation different from that of greater men, except
insofar as salvation is itself hierarchical (which, in Catholic doctrine, it is). However, it seems not to be the case that any one of
the gifts of the Spirit evidently resides in Boromir (unless, perhaps,
discernment at his end); so it cannot quite be said that the Spirit is
fully abroad, even among the Walkers.

One of the few attempts in the first serious years of Tolkien criticism to deal with the theology of *The Lord of the Rings* is a brief
essay by Deborah Webster Rogers, bearing the title "Everyclod
and Everyhero" and ending with the observation that "individually we are hobbits; collectively we are Aragorn." I have elsewhere
observed (in my introduction to *A Tolkien Compass*, 1975) that
Rogers therein hit upon a precise temporal analogue to the doctrine that individually we are humans, while collectively we are the
body of Christ. On reconsideration, though my earlier statement is
certainly true, I am not so sure that this is the right analogue, since
it would apparently make Aragorn a Christ figure, which he is not
(except in the limited sense of embodying the ancient unity of
Prophet, Priest, and King). Nor is he particularly a prefiguring of

Christ (except, it may be, in that unity). It is Gandalf who dies and comes back, not Aragorn, and it is the angels—the messengers—of God (like Gandalf) who take the place of Christ in pre-Christian ages.

We may look briefly at that triad of "Prophet, Priest, and King." Adam was all three, as unfallen Man, and Christ all three, as the New Adam. Melchizedek also, I suppose, and perhaps John the Evangelist after the death of Peter, the Prophet, and James, the Priest. (It was ancient tradition in Asia Minor that the Holy Spirit had been locally resident in John, and we know John was adopted into the Royal family while Christ was on the cross—but this may be somewhat by-the-way here.) I suggest that, precisely as the Adam, when unfallen, was all three, so with Aragorn, still unfallen. In fact, in this moment in the pre-Christian age of a Christian world, that is what we should expect.

I suspect it may be necessary here to examine the implications of the compound "pre-Christian." In one sense, of course, the word has a precise chronological meaning. There was a moment when Christ entered human history, in (owing to a slight Eusebian miscalculation) the year 4 BC (or 4 BCE), and in this sense everything before 4 BC (or 4 BCE) is pre-Christian. But the identity of Jesus the Christ with the *Logos*, the second Person of the pre-existing Trinity, the Divine Son whose Love for and from the Father is Itself the Holy Spirit—this renders the word "pre-Christian," in another sense, entirely meaningless. No Catholic (I should say, no Christian) can imagine our world existing before Christ existed, since He was the Word through Whom all things were made. There was a time before Jesus of Nazareth was born in Bethlehem. But there never was a time before the Second Person of the Trinity existed—only before He was known by us to exist.

Now the chessboard of time on which we live and move is merely the simulacrum of the eternity in which we have our being. The entry of the Christ into human history occurs on that chessboard—but also "before all worlds, God of God, Light of Light, Very God of Very God" (Nicene Creed). It is only the knowledge of Christ (and therefore of the Holy Spirit) that does not exist in pre-Christian times. But Christ exists, and the Spirit also. It is this lack of knowledge—which is dictated by Catholic theology—that has led some observers to think *The Lord of the Rings* an irreligious book. But, as we have said, it is not irreligious: it merely and nec-

essarily portrays a world in which religion is not practiced as we
practice it.

Let me now return to a different and more debatable characteristic of the world: the fact that it is (or may be) prelapsarian, that
there is no inherent tendency toward evil. Granted, this seems to
be the case—but there is no inherent tendency toward good,
either, at least in most places. True, the majority of Hobbits are
only waiting for inspiration to attack the Boss's men. On the other
hand, there is at least misunderstanding abroad: the men of
Gondor distrust (most of them) the Lady in the Wood. There are
Easterlings and Southrons deep and long in evil servitude (III,
280), but there are those who are not. In short, so far as outward
appearances are concerned, it is a world much like ours (these
Easterlings and Southrons might even worship pagan gods in the
way discussed above). But the closer we look—at least the more
inward the look we take—the less like ours it seems. It is a matter
perhaps of "païens ont tort et Chrestiens ont droit": there is a kind
of epic certainty about, and epic gulf between, good and evil. Only
rarely as in Boromir, do the two meet in the same character. Even
Ghân-buri-Ghân is true to Aragorn. Even the King of the Dead is
bound by his oath. (And I am reminded by my friend Bonniejean
Christensen that, in the original edition of *The Hobbit*, even
Gollum plays fair in the riddle game.) If this is a fallen world, the
fall is assuredly incomplete.

What then? Is this an unfallen world? With Morgoth in its history, nameless things gnawing its roots, the Balrog in the abyss,
Sauron mustering his legions, that too seems questionable. I am
driven to conclude that this world is neither quite fallen nor quite
unfallen, and this turns out to be in keeping with a three-directional universe. Middle-earth betwixt Heaven and Hell can be
fallen, to all the round world's four corners. But when Middle-
earth is middle betwixt West and East, the whole round world cannot be fallen (and, in any case, we have noted there is no uttermost
East, no Hell on earth). Moreover, we cannot draw a simple progression from West (Heaven) to East across the map of Tolkien's
Middle-earth. Lothlórien is, after all, east of the Barrow Downs.

But perhaps this is not a fair example, since neither the Barrow
Wights nor the Elves of Lothlórien are men, and it is with men that
we are here concerned. (In another sense, of course, as Humphrey
Carpenter has suggested, Elves might be taken as unfallen Man,

but I do not think this is part of the theology of *The Lord of the Rings*.) Of the other peoples of Middle-earth, apart from those included in the Nine Walkers, only the Ents are not the perversion of the Enemy (according to *The Lord of the Rings*): the Orcs and Trolls were bred by the Enemy in "mockery" of Elves and Ents. And the Ents, while they may become treelike, do not (in *The Lord of the Rings*) lapse into evil (though, curiously trees may: witness Old Man Willow). At least within *The Lord of the Rings* it is only Men and Hobbits (and trees) who are mixed good and evil, and even for Men the West-to-East progression from Good to Evil is not complete, while for Hobbits (and trees) it does not hold at all.

We must reject that supposition and conclude (despite some signs of this West-to-East progression) that the whole of Middle-earth is poised on the brink of the fall. It is angelic presences that have fallen, and some of mankind with them. It is as though Mankind, collectively (to borrow Mrs. Rogers's formulation) is Adam—the old Adam, though not in the colloquial sense: "Male and female created He them, and blessed them, and called their name Adam" (*Genesis* 5:2). And if mankind is Adam—which is what the Hebrew word signifies—then the One Ring, besides all the other things it may be, is the apple of the tree—though an apple of power, not of knowledge. Certainly temptation by the Ring is a common theme of the ring bearer's journey.

It is not, to be sure, the only form of temptation. The *palantiri* tempt also (Pippin, Denethor, Saruman), insofar as they are engines of power. All power tends to corrupt, and absolute power corrupts absolutely. The Ring is the great temptation, as it is the greatest power, and the subsidiary temptations should not blind us to the fact that the presence of this object of temptation in a world not yet fallen but poised on the brink gives a precise theological *locus* for the action: the precise moment in the timeless drama of temptation at which that drama has entered the time scheme of *The Lord of the Rings*. In the terms of our own drama, the apple is being presented to the Man and the Woman, the Serpent (that is, the fallen angel, the rebel) is in the Garden, but no decision has been made. The Adam *may* remain unfallen. (And this, in fact, happens in Lewis's contemporaneous *Perelandra*, published while Tolkien was reading *The Lord of the Rings* to the Inklings.)

I said before that in *The Lord of the Rings* trees may be sentient and moral—or immoral—beings. This fact may explain the inappropriateness of an apple (or any fruit) as the engine of temptation in Tolkien's world. I am not sure the question is of major importance as a matter of theology (it is obviously important as a matter of literary criticism that the object be appropriate), except that it is important that the Ring is capable of providing multiple temptation. An apple, after all, if eaten by an Adam and Eve, could not provide temptation for other men and women, if others existed. But the temptation in *The Lord of the Rings* is multiple: the Adam, as we observed, is collective, even if there is (*pace* Deborah Rogers) no collective Christ.

A while back I noted the problem of reconciling mythic truths in trying to fit the theology of *The Lord of the Rings* in with ours. That statement may have been overly cryptic, and not all the readers may find any need to reconcile theologies—particularly if in their daily world they believe in none, or see no need for any. Yet myth is a kind of obverse side of the coin of theology. And the more we draw the comparisons between Tolkien's world and ours—its temptation, the nature of its timeless moment, its prelapsarian (or its fallen) state—the more we see that Tolkien's theology is that of the Catholic church, as we would expect. But the shutter has been clicked—the exposure taken—at a different point in the process. Indeed, in the end, the Adam does not fall, at least not in the Third Age. Almost, but not quite.

This can be our world only if we can in some way make this part of prelapsarian, pre-Adamite history. Lewis, in *That Hideous Strength*, did just that, in the syncretism I referred to before. When Jane Studdock, in that book, asks where the jewels of St. Anne's come from, she is answered that they are treasures of Logres (which preserves the Númenorean tradition in Britain) from beyond the moon or before the fall. But to do this is to beg a number of questions, one of which (at least) is important here. If we acknowledge this as our world (which Tolkien has indeed said it is), must the temptations of the Ring be part of the Adamite temptation? The answer, I venture to suggest, is *yes*. Of course, *The Lord of the Rings* is not a theological tract, but it is the serious sub-creation of a Catholic and Christian author, presenting an alternative or supplementary mythology to the myth of Eden. And the congruence between the two is worth emphasizing.

Curiously in view of the author's concern for language, it is only Gandalf among the Nine who tames animals with words (and then only Shadowfax). And Gandalf is not part of the Adam. Names are indeed magic in the philologist's world of *The Lord of the Rings*; but—for reasons having more to do perhaps with the paucity of animals than with any doctrine either of theology or of magic—there is little to parallel the myth of the naming day. Yet the Hobbit ponies, and the trees of the Old Forest—and the Barrow Wight, for that matter—do answer to their names when they are called by Iarwain ben-Adar (strange name!), oldest and fatherless, otherwise Tom Bombadil.

Doctrinally I find Tom to be Tolkien's least successful creation within the bounds of *The Lord of the Rings*. Standing alone, he would be a nature spirit, an English woodland presence, both linguistically successful and a substantial artistic achievement. (For all that he was originally a Tolkien family doll.) But he is not standing alone, and it is in this fact that the problem lies. He is not the *genius* (old sense) of the earth, since he is restricted to one part of it—specifically the Tolkienian equivalent of Oxfordshire and Berkshire (Carpenter 1977, p. 182, and we will go further into this in the next chapter). He is apparently a man, since he is clearly not an Elf or a Dwarf or an Ent or a Hobbit or one of the fallen races, but he is not one of the Men of the West. I suppose one could save appearances by making him an angel, of a different order from the *Istari*, or by making him a god, but in both cases we would seem to be in conflict with Tolkien's mythology.

Perhaps we might make Tom a man, the untempted part of Tolkien's multiple Adam, and see in him one further way of treating the Ring. If the Ring is the Adam's temptation, Tom is that part of the Adam that, in primal innocence, does not feel the temptation. Though I find him an anomalous creation, I can make shift to account for him theologically—but only with the uneasy feeling that making shift is all I am doing. (Since the first edition of this book appeared, this statement has been criticized by a number of readers who simply don't see the problem: perhaps their understanding of theological consistency—or even of theology—is unlike mine, or perhaps they place less or no importance on it. But perhaps they may see a part of the problem in the fact that Treebeard is "eldest" and Tom "oldest and fatherless"—but what of that strange name "ben-Adar"?)

Let me turn now to another theological question, on prayer and mediation. That *The Lord of the Rings* provides us with a world in which prayer is made only to intermediaries—and particularly to Elbereth of the Elves—is clear. If God is the Unknown God, direct prayer to Him would, of course, be ruled out (only in desperation, and probably then only in our fallen world, are prayers directed "To Whom It May Concern"). But even the prayer to Elbereth is almost entirely unlike prayer in our world, or at least as we generally conceive it to be here. For one thing, it works immediately and obviously. For another, it is more an invocation of a name than a petition. (Of course, this ties in with the magic of naming, and with our own world's historic or prehistoric connection between names and religion, as in Julian Jaynes, *The Origins of Consciousness in the Breakdown of the Bicameral Mind*—one of Owen Barfield's favorites.) But even when the men of Gondor bow towards Númenor before meals, they are bowing, not praying.

This has to do, I think, with the nature of the mediation between God and humankind. The world of *The Lord of the Rings* has not yet seen the coming of the one Mediator (and Advocate) Jesus Christ, and with Him, His prayer. The power of God passes from Erú to the Valar to the Eldar to Men. (There is some irregularity in the process, as well as a problem with speaking of the Elves as unfallen, given Fëanor's actions as recounted in appendix A, but these do not destroy the argument.) The Elves, though they can be tempted, mediate the power of God, though not directly—and they do it not by virtue of office, as a priest, but by virtue of Elfhood. Or do they? Galadriel, after all, is great among Elvenkind, by virtue of her rank at creation and thus, we might say, her office. We have in this world no priests, but have we a priesthood? There are no formal sacraments (though there is certainly a sacramental quality to some of the meals, as Pippin's with Denethor), but are we in a sacramental world?

The outward and visible sign of an inward and spiritual grace— that, it will be recalled, is the definition of a sacrament in the catechism. It is also virtually an exact description of Tolkien's world and of Tolkien's art (in which even the use of language is sacramental—in fact, as we noted, quite in keeping with early medieval ideas of the Sacrament of the Word). The triumphant language in which triumph is recounted is an outward and visible sign of what is happening within. The exterior beauty of the Elves embodies— perhaps it would be better to say "bodies forth"—an interior beauty. Orcs and Trolls and evil men are foul to look upon. When

Saruman dies, his true character, masked by his arts in his life, is finally revealed. We are in fact engaged in a continuous process of minding true things by what their appearances be. And when appearances ("looking foul") do not truly represent an inward and spiritual grace ("being fair"), as with Aragorn as Strider, that fact is worthy not only of comment but of verse ("All that is gold does not glitter"). We are indeed in a sacramental world, to answer the second question posed in the last paragraph. (Has it been noted, by the way, that one of the most widely-played rock songs of all time twists this verse—"All that glitters is gold"—in setting up an opposition between the world of the 1970s and what is essentially a Tolkienian vision of the May Queen? The song is, of course, Led Zeppelin's "Stairway to Heaven.")

This matter of the sacramental vision (including the Sacrament of the Word), I believe, implies an answer to the first question, whether this world has a priesthood. In our own world, in our epoch, the priesthood (whether of Aaron or Melchizedek) is specifically ordained and differentiated from the nations not so ordained. One could argue that only in a fallen (that is, nonsacramental) world would there be this kind of priesthood or the need for it. In an unfallen world, any unfallen Man, or Elf, or Dwarf (perhaps), or Ent, or Hobbit could mediate divinity. Just as all acts could be sacramental, so all men (and Elves, at least) could have the power of Christ and of Peter. Just as the fallen creatures (or perhaps "spoiled" is better) could mediate the diabolical.

It will be noted that I say "could"—the acts *could* be sacramental, the men and Elves *could* have the power. It is not certain that they would. It is not at all certain that the world, if unfallen, would remain so. Indeed, after completing *The Lord of the Rings* (if I have the chronology right), Tolkien went on to a planned sequel in which, about a hundred years into the Fourth Age, boredom set in, humankind being unable to stand prosperity for any considerable period of time. (It is this period in which, if I were writing a story in Tolkien's world, I would place that story, though of course if I were to write such a story, it could use none of Tolkien's names, nor mention his.) I think it important, nonetheless, that Tolkien feigned (if it would be feigning) that temptation, having been conquered in the form of the Ring, started again in a new form.

Our own mythology makes the decision to eat the apple, the temptation and the succumbing to temptation, almost instantaneous. Tolkien's mythology makes it a long haul, *per saecula saeculorum*. Because the Adam, once fallen, could not rise again unaided, we tend to think of the great temptation as a kind of "one-shot deal": once resisted, it would not come again. Lewis's *Perelandra* seems to be presenting this doctrine. But so far as I know, there is no reason to assume this would necessarily be the case. Our own experience in a fallen world—unending temptation—cannot be used as evidence here, nor (*per contra*) can the fact that Christ made one oblation of Himself (once offered) be used to support the view that the Adam, once having surmounted temptation, would not have been tempted again. This is a matter not so much of received doctrine as of imagination: here, in other words, Tolkien's artistry is at work. It would appear that the Tempter we have always with us—the Prince, we might even think, of this World.

That Tolkien's is a world mostly without gods and certainly without churches or temples—note the connection of the Hallows with kingship rather than priesthood—turns out to have reasons both profoundly theological and essentially Christian. That the sacred places thus depend on kingship might seem to introduce a political question, but to call it political would be to impose the categories of a fallen world on one unfallen. This, by the way is a point from time to time overlooked in discussions of Tolkien's politics. He was, I believe, a Tory, and the Shire is a Tory Democrat's paradise. But kingship by divine grace, if not divine right, is theologically necessary in a prelapsarian universe, or at least in a Christian prelapsarian universe.

Let me turn to another matter. Theologians have for years distinguished the four cardinal virtues from the three theological virtues. Prudence, temperance, justice, and fortitude are supposed to be common to all systems (part of the *Tao*, in Lewis's terms), while faith, hope, and charity—or love (*caritas, agapé*)—are Christian. The same theologians have distinguished between mortal ("deadly") and venial sins, eventually agreeing upon seven of the former: lust, envy, pride, sloth (*accidie*), gluttony, avarice (greed), and anger. It may be worthwhile here to examine Tolkien's universe according to these traditional heptarchies. If this is a pre-Christian world, but not prelapsarian, we should expect to find only the four cardinal virtues and all seven of the deadly sins. If it is a prelapsarian world, we should expect to find all seven virtues, and only one of the sins should be deadly: the sin against the Holy Spirit.

As we would expect, we find all seven virtues. Recall the constant emphasis on prudence for the Walkers and the Elven counsel of temperance to Gimli in the matter of the waybread. Recall the justice of the King to Beregond and the fortitude of the Hobbits. We have already noted the faith of the Nine (except Boromir) and we could as easily have noted their hope. And for the greatest of these seven, charity (*agapé*), we need only recall Frodo's giving his life for the Shire: "I tried to save the Shire, and it has been saved, but not for me. It must often be so, Sam, when things are in danger: some one has to give them up, lose them, so that others may keep them" (III, 382). Beside this may be set Christ's pronouncement in the New Testament: "Greater love than this hath no man, that a man lay down his life for his friends."

Of the deadly sins, we find no lust, no envy except among Orcs, a tendency to avarice among Dwarves perhaps (but not in Gimli), little sloth, not much gluttony, some anger (Sam, against Gollum, with ill results), and a considerable amount of pride. It seems almost as though pride holds a special place among the seven, a kind of extra deadliness in Tolkien's world. And so it does. Now, pride is (our theologians tell us) the sin against the Holy Spirit. Thus it is altogether fitting, within the framework of Catholic theology, that in a world informed by the Spirit, the one mortal sin should be the sin against the Spirit. All sins represent the exaltation of the self over others, but pride intrudes the self not merely in the relations of man (or woman) to man (or woman), but directly into the relations of man with God. It will be remembered that pride was Lucifer's sin and (in wanting to be as gods) the Adam's. It is the sin that brought about the fall, and thus it is the sin, above all others, to be found in a tempted unfallen world.

Whichever theological road of inquiry we take thus seems to lead us to the same point. The intersection of the timeless moment with time in *The Lord of the Rings* is at the temptation of the Adam. So long as the Adam is unfallen, this remains the point of intersection, with no need for the redemption. Like us, Tolkien's characters must continually surmount temptation; unlike us, they have no predisposition to succumb. (This brings us back, I think, to the "fairy-tale" morality that Walter Scheps has argued is inapplicable to our own world; it is, however, perfectly—indeed, uniquely—applicable to the world of *The Lord of the Rings*.)

As I said before, Tolkien has not written a theological tract: his dislike of allegory in all its manifestations would alone be enough to make that unlikely even if there were not a series of other reasons for not considering *The Lord of the Rings* in that light. Chief among those other reasons is the long, slow growth of Tolkien's creation from language to myth to action. But it remains true, and important, that his creation is theologically in accord with Catholic doctrine. That fact explains not only the sometimes unsatisfactory results for psychological review of *The Lord of the Rings*, but also the lack of "religion" in Tolkien's world. Theology, in effect, preempts religion.

I have suggested that this is paradoxical, but why would it be? This age of charismatic Christianity, baptism in the Spirit, speaking in tongues, and healing—this seems not, after all, to be such an unlikely field for Pauline theology to take root in. I agree. However, Tolkien's *magnum opus* is the creation not of this present age but of the time from 1914 to 1954—with, as I have suggested, roots before 1914. It certainly cannot be claimed that *The Lord of the Rings* produced this charismatic revival: I strongly doubt it had anything to do with it. It cannot be claimed that the two have the same efficient cause: whatever produced the revival, it was not Edwardian literature, English philology, or the Birmingham Oratory. (Nor even, I suggest, have they the same proximate cause.) In short, *The Lord of the Rings* was created in Freud's heyday in a sort of splendid isolation from the psychological world. Our institutions, our popular press, and our television shows mirror Freud. But we read *The Lord of the Rings*. (I wonder, in this connection, if it is coincidental that the quarter-century, almost, between the two editions of this study has seen the growth of attachment theory and "narratization" therapy at the expense, to some degree, of orthodox Freudianism.)

There is at least one loose end to tie up here, and that is the ultimate fate of the races of Middle-earth. To Men (and Hobbits) is given the gift, or doom, of men: to pass beyond the circles of the world, in death and resurrection. To Elves is given immortality but not in Middle-earth. The Dwarves are clearly tied to Middle-earth, but *The Lord of the Rings* gives us no clues (that I have found) to their possible resurrection, or any other form of immortality (except that Gimli achieves an Elven immortality). The Ents, I suppose, go either with Elves or Men—certainly, as we noted, Treebeard and Galadriel will meet again, which in fact suggests that they go with the Elves. Presumably Orcs and Trolls will perish with their maker, everlastingly. Let me repeat that I am here restricting myself to *The Lord of the Rings*. Tolkien's theology is more fully developed in *The Silmarillion* (still more fully in *The History of Middle-earth*), but I am looking here, as I have said, at *The Lord of the Rings*, to see what can be gained from it.

"Without doubt they shall perish everlastingly." That line from the Athanasian Creed provides a Catholic definition of Hell, and one that fits into Tolkien's world. (It is, I suggest, a very powerful, and frightening, line.) In our fallen days, the punishment of evil is timeless—Hell reaches back, so to speak, and infects even the former pleasures of the damned—just as the reward for good is timeless. But in an unfallen world—one whose timeless moment is before, not after, the succumbing to temptation—Evil, however personified, cannot have a permanent habitation within the circles of the world. As humankind triumphs everlastingly over temptation (however much by the skin of our teeth)—and this will, by definition, be happening so long as there is no Fall—Evil must perish everlastingly. The world is not symmetrical because, in fact, Evil continually falls off the edge of the world. Though the gods—that is, the Valar—do not decree that it shall cease ever to have been, the decisions of Men, and Elves, and Hobbits, at least in the Third Age, will decree that it shall cease to be. Everlastingly.

And so it shall be—at least until it creeps in again in the Next Age. The First Age ended with the Great Battle, in which the Host of Valinor broke Thangorodrim and overthrew Morgoth. Then most of the Noldor returned unto the Far West and dwelt in Eressëa within sight of Valinor; and many of the Sindar went over sea also (III, 452). The Second Age ended with the first overthrow of Sauron, the servant of Morgoth, and the taking of the One Ring. Sauron was overthrown by Elendil and Gil-galad, who perished. Isildur took the One Ring. Sauron passed away and the Ringwraiths went into the Shadows (III, 452, 455). The Third Age came to its end in the War of the Rings, though the Fourth Age was not held to have begun until the departure of Master Elrond from Middle-earth. On March 25th (Lady Day, celebrated through our Middle Ages as the birth of Christ and the beginning of the world—and to be the Last Day), Third Age year 3019, the One Ring fell into the Cracks of Doom; Barad-dûr was fallen, and Sauron passed away—again. But it was not until September 29 (the Feast of St. Michael and All Angels in our Middle Ages), Third Age year 3021, that the Third Age came to an end. The Fellowship of the Ring lasted into the Fourth Age, for in the year 120 of the Fourth Age, "on March 1st came at last the passing of King Elessar. It is said that the beds of Meriadoc and Peregrin were set beside the bed of the Great King. Then Legolas built a grey ship in Ithilien, and sailed down Anduin and so over Sea; and with him, it is said, went Gimli the Dwarf. And when that ship passed an end was come in Middle-earth of the fellowship of the Ring" (III, 452, 467–68, 472). And that, clearly, is the elegiac note of Malory and the passing of the Table Round—in a world where (to use our names) the Christian King Arthur defeats the rebel Mordred.

Morgoth was shut away leaving Sauron and the Balrogs behind. Sauron was defeated, his realm—and indeed he himself—ended. But the seeds Morgoth planted grow and grow again, as his work is defeated and defeated again. And Sauron's also, I suspect. There is no rest. But there is victory—certainly at the end of an age—and with that, within the circles of the world, we must be content. If that victory had continued, if our world was still at that timeless moment, our sacraments would not be confined to churches, nor our God to Sundays—and we would see *The Lord of the Rings* as a godly book, if not a religious one.

4

In the Far Northwest of the Old World

My road calls me, lures me
West, east, south, and north;
Most roads lead men homewards,
My road leads me forth.

—JOHN MASEFIELD

And not by eastern windows only,
When daylight comes, comes in the light.
In front the sun climbs slow, how slowly,
But westward, look, the land is bright.

—ARTHUR HUGH CLOUGH

That *The Lord of the Rings* is set in the Northwest of the Old World there is no doubt, and I have no doubt that the setting is important—for two reasons. First of all, this is Tolkien's own country, the England for which he so earnestly desired to create (or sub-create) a mythology. We recall that in the very beginning of *The Lord of the Rings*, in part 1 of the prologue, "Concerning Hobbits," that the days of the Third Age of Middle-earth, "are now long past, and the shape of all lands has been changed; but the regions in which Hobbits lived then were doubtless the same as those in which they still linger: the North-west of the old World, east of the sea" (I, 21).

Second, both North and West have a significance—
significatio—though I hasten to add that, so far as I can see, the
significance of the Northwest is simply the significance of the
North and the West, and not some superadded "synergistic" compound. When Frodo says Strider is only a Ranger, Gandalf replies
"My dear Frodo, that is just what the Rangers are; the last remnant
in the *North* of the great people, the men of the *West*" (I, 291,
emphasis mine). We should begin, I think, with the dominant
myth (if you will forgive me the word)—that is, the myth of the
West. We have already discussed Tolkien's three-directional universe, and the great goodness attaching to the West. Let me briefly
summarize what we have said, and then go on to say at least a little more.

We have remarked that Aragorn is one of the Men of the West,
long-lived, of Elven descent, and "of the blood of the West unmingled," King by right and inheritance. We have remarked the conversation of Treebeard with Celeborn and Galadriel, in which they
say that they will meet again not in Middle-earth, but in the land
of Tasarinan. We have noted that the meeting is not to take place
in Middle-earth, *and* it is not to take place until Númenor is raised
up. It will indeed take place in Númenor. We might think
Númenor would be part of any Middle-earth, as (we might think)
would be any Isles of the Blest, but it is not part of Tolkien's
Middle-earth.

If the West is Heaven (or Paradise), then the East in some sense
approaches Hell, even though the symmetry is incomplete, and
Middle-earth is middle because betwixt West and East. This reading fits in with the land under the wave and Middle-earth as separate entities: by it, the Undying Lands remain forever beyond the
circles of the world, reachable only by the Old Straight Track. By
it, Númenor (or, rather, the Isle of Elenna) will be raised up, the
world—Middle-earth being included in the circles of the world—
will be changed, and the dead will be raised (III, 428). This is the
framework, but in my reading over *The Lord of the Rings* in preparation for writing this chapter (would it be for the fortieth time, or
more?), one thing has struck me with particular force. We are
introduced to this, as to much else in the background of *The Lord
of the Rings*, by hints and slight mentions, over the three volumes.
It is certainly part of Tolkien's mythology for England, and his
desire for the fair elusive beauty that some call Celtic. It is unques-

tionably based on the Celtic Islands of the Blest, on Hy Bréasaíl, on the drowned lands of Lyonesse, on all the westering motion of the sacred in Celtic lore, on the *imramm* (and he himself published an "Imram" in 1955). But he does not here tell much of the myth (until he gets to the appendices): it is almost as though, by knowing the myth (if we do), we discover it here, underlying and informing the story, until we reach the appendices.

In the opening chapters, in the Shire, we find Bilbo and Gandalf "sitting at the open window of a small room looking out west on to the garden" (I, 49). The link of garden with west, though minor, is fitting (to cross mythologies, the gardens of Ponemah, perhaps?). Then, while things are beginning to stir, around the time of Frodo's fiftieth birthday, there is this report from Sam:

> "And I've heard tell the Elves are moving west. They do say they are going to the harbours, out away beyond the White towers." Sam waved his arm vaguely; neither he nor any of them knew how far it was to the Sea, past the old towers beyond the western borders of the Shire. But it was an old tradition that away over there stood the Grey Havens, from which at times elven-ships set sail, never to return. "They are sailing, sailing, sailing over the Sea, they are going into the West and they are leaving us," said Sam, half chanting the words, shaking his head sadly and solemnly. (I, 74)

Then, when Gandalf begins to tell Frodo the story of the One Ring (I, 83), he tells him of the Men of Westernesse, elf-friends: "The strength of the Elves to resist [Sauron] was greater long ago; and not all Men were estranged from them. The Men of Westernesse came to their aid. . . . It was Gil-galad Elven-king and Elendil of Westernesse who overthrew Sauron, though they themselves perished in the deed." When the hobbits hear the High Elves singing (I, 117), the song begins with the lines, "Snow-white, Snow-white! O Lady clear! / O Queen beyond the Western Seas!" and ends "O Elbereth! Gilthoniel! / We still remember, we who dwell / In this far land beneath the trees, / Thy starlight on the Western Seas." The linking of the Elves with the West is made, and made again.

Of course, the west (no capital W) may simply be part of a proverbial saying, as in "east or west all woods must fail" (I, 159). But even Tom Bombadil (I, 201) tells the hobbits of the Men of

Westernesse, and when they meet with Strider at the Prancing Pony, he speaks of the "Shadow in the East" (I, 229). The opposition of West and East grows clearer. The *Forsaken Inn* is a day's journey *east* of Bree (I, 253). And when Strider comes up to Bilbo and Frodo in Rivendell (I, 306–7), Bilbo calls him Dúnadan. "'Why do you call him Dúnadan?' asked Frodo. '*The* Dúnadan,' said Bilbo. 'He is often called that here. But I thought you knew enough Elvish to know *dún-adan*: Man of the West, Númenorean.'" And when the Council of Elrond discusses what to do with the Ring (I, 349), Galdor remarks that his heart tells him that Sauron will expect them to take the Western way— whereas, of course, the way they take is to the East, to destroy the Ring where it was made.

It is, I think, revealing, that the Elven songs in their lines (and especially their concluding lines) come so often to the West: we have quoted one, and here is another. "But from the west has come no word, / And on the Hither Shore / No tidings Elven-folk have heard / Of Amroth ever more" (I, 442). And another (though here not in the concluding lines): "*Andúne pella Vardo tellumar / nu luini yassen tintilar i eleni / ómaryo airetári-lírinen*" ("beyond the West beneath the blue vaults of Varda wherein the stars tremble in the song of her voice, holy and queenly"—I, 489). And, of course, when Galadriel declines the Ring, "'I pass the test,' she said. 'I will diminish, and go into the West, and remain Galadriel'" (I, 474). And just to be sure there is no doubt, when they are going down the Great River that divides Osgiliath, and Legolas shoots the great black winged creature, "it fell out of the air, vanishing down into the gloom of the eastern shore" (I, 501). And "the Enemy holds the eastern bank" of the river, and "the Orcs prowl on the east shore" (I, 504, 505).

I have not, of course, touched on every reference to West or East (or even west or east) in *The Fellowship of the Ring*, but I have not missed a great number of them, either. The line is clearly drawn, and the link of the Elves and the west well-forged, but it has scarcely been dinned into our ears, at least in the first two books (book 1 and book 2 make up *The Fellowship of the Ring*, volume I of *The Lord of the Rings*,). In the next two (books 3 and 4, making up the second volume of *The Lord of the Rings*, *The Two Towers*), the number of references is scarcely greater, though one may add in some countervailing references to the East. In

Aragorn's apostrophe to Gondor (II, 29), apparently an Elvish invocation, he asks, "O! Gondor, Gondor! Shall Men behold the Silver Tree, Or West Wind blow again between the Mountains and the Sea?" When Merry and Pippin are talking to Treebeard, he remarks, on the changing times, "Mordor is a long way away. But it seems that the wind is setting East, and the withering of all woods may be drawing near" (II, 95). We note also that the songs of the Ents about the Entwives "have not come west over the Mountains to the Shire" (II, 98), reminding us that the Shire is indeed not only in the North but also in the West of Middle-earth. And then (II, 101, 102) we hear an Elvish song of the Ents and Entwives, how "When woodland hills are green and cool, and wind is in the West, / Come back to me! Come back to me, and say my land is best" and then, in the final strophe, "Together we will take the road that leads into the West, / And far away may find a land where both our hearts may rest." Once again, this is the West as seen by the Elves.

Not all references to east or west are fully relevant here. When Legolas says (II, 121) that if they had left the Great Plain and struck west on the second or third day they would have struck Fangorn together, that is *west* but not *West*. Even when the Sun falls down the sky into the West in a great fire and blood-red burning (II, 139), it is the West (the sacred direction), but not a reference, we might say, to the True West, and the same holds, I believe, when (II, 140) the waxing moon sinks into the cloudy West. Then we have a curious form of the legend or *mythos* of the West, as among the Men of Rohan, in the song of the Rohirrim that Aragorn sings (II, 143), "The days have gone down in the West behind the hills into shadow, / Who shall gather the smoke of the dead wood burning, / Or behold the flowing years from the Sea returning?" I call this curious because it may be a combination of the fact that the day (the sun) sinks into the west, and the idea of the sacred West taken over from the Men of Gondor, *Dúnedain*—as the Saxons might have taken over such a thing from the Celts. But it is not the story of the Men of the West, unmingled. Yet in context, though "pagan," it has at least a suggestion of it.

Theoden, regaining his life, stands with Gandalf, "and together they looked out from the high place toward the East," while "doom hangs still on a thread" (II, 154). When Shadowfax bears

Gandalf, and Éomer cries out "Were the breath of the West Wind to make a body visible, even so would it appear," there again the West is both the significant (if "pagan") direction for the Rohirrim, and the sacred West of the *Dúnedaín* (II, 164), nor is it accidental that the Rohirrim under Théoden ride West (II, 165)—"*Westú Théoden hál!*" On the other hand, the speech of the Dunlendings "once was spoken in many western valleys of the Mark" (II, 180)—but that was because the Dunlendings were there when Eorl the Young came to the aid of Gondor and was given their eastlands (where the unfaithful Dunlendings dwelt), whose western border was the Westfold from which Erkenbrand rides with Gandalf Mithrandir (II, 186). And then we come to Isengard—"long had it been beautiful; and there great lords had dwelt, the Wardens of Gondor upon the West, and wise men that watched the stars" (II, 204). But Isengard was not its only name: its citadel was Orthanc, "the name of which had (by design or chance) a twofold meaning; for in the Elvish speech *orthanc* signifies Mount Fang, but in the language of the Mark of old the cunning mind" (II, 204)—a double word or meaning, in two languages (one from the West), rather like Eärendil.

So much for book 3, and when we get into book 4 we can expect fewer references to the West or the west, for this is Sam and Frodo going into the Land of Mordor. But we can expect references to the East (or east), which may, after all, be taken as implicit references to the West (or west). "A chill wind blew from the East" as Sam and Frodo stood on the brink of a tall cliff, after "they had worked steadily eastward," and now "South and east they stared" (II, 265). There are orcs, out prowling on the east bank of the river (II, 266). Frodo tells Sam (II, 267) he feels "all naked on the east side." Trees were dead and gaunt, "bitten to the core by the eastern winds" (II, 268). Then, in a line that reminds us of what is at the anthropological root (so to speak) of the Celtic West, the "hurrying darkness, now gathering great speed, rushed up from the East and swallowed the sky" (II, 270).

But after the storm has passed, clear sky "was growing in the East once more" (II, 273). What that clear sky presages just then we do not know, but even in the East there may be a signal of hope. What comes next is Gollum, who clenches "his long hand into a bony fleshless knot, shaking it towards the East" (II, 282).

When Frodo and Sam are with Gollum, in the passage of the marshes, they all three shrink from the Ringwraith. But Gollum shrinks also from the white-face moon, until she goes down, "westering far beyond Tol Brandir" (II, 300): we know—though he does not—that the moon and the Ringwraiths are enemies, not friends. And when (II, 312) they are looking at the roads to the Gate of Mordor, they run northwards and eastwards and southwards: the southwards road runs briefly west ("Westward, to his right, it turned"), but then "southwards into the deep shadows." Frodo sees "Men of other race, out of the wide Eastlands, gathering to the summons of their Overlord" (II, 313). The hobbits take refuge in a little valley, a dell: "the sun moved, until at last the shadow of the western rim of their dell grew long"—and then, the "dark was deep when at length they set out, creeping over the westward rim of the dell" (II, 324), as though toward the sun's destination (though in fact they go eastward toward Mordor). And Sam is heartened, when "he saw the sun rise out of the reek, or haze, or dark shadow, or whatever it was, that lay ever to the east, and it sent its golden beams down upon the trees and glades about him" (334).

When Frodo and Sam encounter Faramir, they go with him to Henneth Annûn, the Window of the Sunset, facing west, where his men are gathered, their refuge and place of strength (II, 358). They come to table with Faramir and his men. "Before they ate, Faramir and all his men turned and faced west in a moment of silence" (II, 361). But otherwise, while they are with Faramir, they go neither west nor east, though they look to the West.

Even when they take up their weary journey again, while Gollum mutters "Long way to go still, south and east" (II, 387), they see, as a sign, their first night again on the road, the Mountains of Gondor, glowing, "remote in the West, under a fire-flecked sky" (II, 387). Under Gollum's guidance, they work "eastwards, up the dark sloping land" (II, 389). In the morning, "no day came. . . . In the East there was a dull red glare under the lowering cloud" (II, 390). Then, the "red glare over Mordor died way. The twilight deepened as great vapours rose in the East" (II, 391). And when Gollum has led them to the Stairs of Cirith Ungol, reluctantly, "Frodo turned his back on the West and followed as his guide led him, out into the darkness of the East" (II, 396). At the Bridge, when the Wraith King is seeking the hobbits, he turns away in haste. "Already the hour had struck, and at his great master's bidding he must march with war into the West" (II, 401). Sauron looks toward the West, where he does not belong, which is not his, while slowly, step by step, the Ringbearer moves ever Eastward. "Big things going on away west," as Shagrat the orc says to Gorbag the orc, but "in the meantime enemies have got up the stairs" (II, 442).

Then, in the fifth book (at the beginning of *The Return of the King*), we are back westward with the rest of the Company, and as we might expect, the references to the West and to the west both increase. Pippin (III, 20) catches a "glimpse of high white peaks . . . as they caught the light of the westering moon" (note the contrast with Gollum). "Anduin, going in a wide knee about the hills of Emyn Arnen in South Ithilien, bent sharply west" (III, 23, and one might think, "bent sharply West"). As Pippin looks out over morning and the world (III, 40), there is promise of what is coming in a "stiffening breeze from the East." "Things move in the far East, beyond the Inland Sea" (III, 43). The last succoring troops enter the citadel, and "in the West the dying sun had set all the fume on fire, and now Mindolluin stood black against a burning smoulder flecked with embers" (50).

"The night was old and the East grey" when Merry and Legolas and Gimli "rode up at last from Deeping Coomb and came back to the Hornburg" (III, 56). Aragorn takes the Paths of the Dead and comes ere midnight the third day to the Stone of Erech. Of which "those who still remembered the lore of Westernesse told that it had been brought out of the ruin of Númenor and set there by Isildur at his landing" (III, 74). Merry rides to Dunharrow with Théoden, who tells him "Long years in the space of days it seems since I rode west," and they come down into the valley "where the Snowbourn flowed near the western walls of the dale, and . . . [so] the King of the Mark came back victorious out of the West to Dunharrow" (III, 78). It has occurred to me that "the hobbit on his little shaggy grey pony, and the Lord of Rohan on his great white horse" (III, 77) recapitulate Ceddie Errol on his pony and the Earl of Dorincourt on his great horse in *Little Lord Fauntleroy*, which was of course an omnipresent vision in the world of Tolkien's youth.

At Dunharrow, he is met by the chieftain Dúnhere. "At dawn three days ago . . . Shadowfax came like a wind out of the west to

Edoras, and Gandalf brought tidings of your victory" (III, 79). Some out of the great concourse of men gathered at the Dunharrow hail "the king and the riders from the West with glad cries" (III, 79), but it is still a solemn and quiet assembly for the war coming out of the East. At the Siege of Gondor (III, 114), though "the enemy was checked, and for the moment driven back, great forces were flowing in from the East." There are "Men of a new sort . . . broad and grim, bearded like dwarves, wielding great axes. Out of some savage land in the East they have come, we deem" (III, 115). They despair for Rohan, but (III, 126), "Horns, horns, horns. In dark Mindolluin's sides they dimly echoed. Great horns of the north wildly blowing. Rohan had come at last." Rohan is guided by old Ghán through the Stonewain Valley, while "eastward and southward the slopes were bare and rocky" (III, 132).

Then, as Rohan had come in the hour beyond hope, there comes a greater. For

> upon the foremost ship a great standard broke. . . . There flowered a White Tree, and that was for Gondor; but Seven Stars were about it, and a high crown above it, the signs of Elendil that no lord had borne for years beyond count. . . . Thus came Aragorn son of Arathorn, Elessar, Isildur's heir, out of the Paths of the Dead, borne upon a wind from the sea to the kingdom of Gondor. . . . East rode the knights of Dol Amroth driving the enemy before them. . . . South strode Éomer and men fled before his face. . . . There came Legolas and Gimli wielding his axe, and Halbarad with the standard, and Elladan and Elrohir with stars on their brow, and the dour-handed Dûnedain, Rangers of the North, leading a great valour of the folk of Lebennin and Lamedon and the fiefs of the South. But before all went Aragorn with the Flame of the West, Andúril like a new fire kindled, Narsil re-forged as deadly as of old; and upon his brow was the Star of Elendil. (III, 150)

When Merry and Éowyn are in the Houses of Healing, injured by the Enemy's weapons, awaiting Aragorn's coming, "soon they began to fall down into darkness, and as the sun turned west, a grey shadow crept over their faces" (III, 136). But even now, and even as they begin their healing, we are all awaiting the last throw. "Two days later the army of the West was all assembled on the Pelennor" (III, 195). On the third day out from Minas Tirith, the army began its northward march. "The weather of the world remained fair, and the wind held in the west, but nothing could waft away the glooms and the sad mists that clung about the Mountains of Shadow" (III, 198). And then we are back with Frodo and Sam, and they see the darkness breaking up out in the world. "It was the morning of the fifteenth of March, and over the vale of Anduin the Sun was rising above the eastern shadow, and the southwest wind was blowing. Théoden lay dying on the Pelennor Fields" (III, 240). As Sam and Frodo crawl ever closer to their goal, they take the northward road, "maybe the way their hunters would least expect them to take" (III, 241), avoiding the direct eastward road. As they move slowly along, they see that on "its outer marges under the westward mountains Mordor was a dying land, but it was not yet dead" (III, 243).

It is not long after that the "wind of the world blew now from the West, and the great clouds were lifted high, floating away eastward; but still only a grey light came to the dreary fields of Gorgoroth" (III, 245). As they climb Mount Doom, in "the morning a grey light came again, for in the high regions the west wind still blew, but down on the stones behind the fences of the Black Land the air seemed almost dead" (III, 258). The desperate journey goes on, as the Ring goes south and the banners of the kings ride north, and there "came at last a dreadful nightfall; and even as the Captains of the West drew near to the end of the living lands, the two wanderers came to an hour of blank despair" (III, 261). They "could not follow this road any longer; for it went on eastward into the Great Shadow" (III, 262). Finally Sam looks down on Sauron's Road to the Sammath Naur: "Out of the Dark Tower's huge western gate it came" (III, 269). Over this road Sam carries Frodo,: "after climbing eastward for some time it bent back upon itself at a sharp angle and went westward for a space" (III, 271), and in that westward space, Gollum returns to them, and his attack spurs Frodo on to the Crack of Doom—where, finally, as we know, he fulfills his mission, and the Ring falls into the Crack of Doom (or rather, Gollum falls into the Crack, holding the Ring).

Gandalf

lifted up his arms and called once more in a clear voice. "Stand, Men of the West! Stand and wait! This is the hour of doom." And even as he spoke the earth rocked beneath their feet. Then rising swiftly up, far above the Towers of the Black Gate, high above the mountains, a vast soaring darkness sprang into the sky, flickering with fire. The earth groaned and quaked. The Towers of the teeth swayed, tottered, and fell down; the mighty rampart trembled; the Black Gate was hurled in ruin. . . . "The realm of Sauron is ended!" said Gandalf. "The ring-bearer has fulfilled his Quest." . . . The Captains bowed their heads, and when they looked up again, behold, their enemies were flying. . . . But the Men of Rhûn and of Harad, Easterling and Southron, saw the ruin of their war and the great majesty and glory of the Captains of the West. And those that were deepest and longest in evil servitude, hating the West, and yet were men proud and bold, in turn now gathered themselves for a last stand. (III, 279–80)

One particularly interesting reference to the East comes when Éowyn complains to Faramir that her window in the Houses of Healing does not look eastward (III, 294). This is after we (but not they) have learned of the destruction of Sauron, and we have here, I think, both a precognition—or recognition—of that destruction and, still more perhaps, a looking toward the sunrise (even, it may be, the sunrise of the new age). It is a short while later that the Eagle, flying (and is this really an αγγελος = *angelos* = angel?), bears "tidings beyond hope to the Lords of the West," commanding "Sing and be glad, all ye children of the West, / for your king shall come again, / and he shall dwell among you, / all the days of your life" (III, 297–98).

When he has been crowned, Aragorn tells Gandalf that he would, if he could, still have his counsel, but Gandalf tells him, "The burden must lie now upon you and your kindred" (III, 308). To which Aragorn replies, "But I shall die. . . . For I am a mortal man, though being what I am, and of the race of the West unmingled, I may have life far longer than other men, yet that is but a little while; and when those who are now in the wombs of women are born and have grown old, I too shall grow old" (III, 308). And die. And so will Arwen, who has chosen the doom of Lúthien, not to go into the West, "But in my stead you shall go, Ring-bearer, when the time comes, and if you then desire it. If your hurts grieve you still and the memory of your burden is heavy, then you may pass into the West, until all your wounds and weariness are healed" (III, 312). Until that time, as Aragorn tells Frodo, for him "in all the lands of the West there will ever be a welcome" (III, 311).

The North (where the line of Isildur has been preserved) and West (where it now reigns) are linked in the great pageant before Midsummer's Day.

> It was the day before Midsummer when messengers came from Amon Dîn to the City, and they said there was a riding of fair folk out of the North, and they drew near now to the walls of the Pelennor. And the King said: "At last they have come. Let all the City be made ready!" Upon the very Eve of Midsummer, when the sky was blue as sapphire and white stars opened in the East, but the West was still golden, and the air was cool and fragrant, the riders came down the North-way to the gates of Minas Tirith. First rode Elrohir and Elladan with a banner of silver, then came Glorfindel and Erestor and all the household of Rivendell, and after them came the Lady Galadriel and Celeborn, Lord of Lothlórien, riding upon white steeds and with them many fair folk of their land, grey-cloaked with white gems in their hair; and last came Master Elrond, mighty among Elves and Men, bearing the sceptre of Annúminas, and beside him on a grey palfrey rode Arwen his daughter, Evenstar of her people. (309–10)

When the travelers ride back on the North-way, the hobbits with them, they "had journeyed thus far by the west-ways, for they had much to speak of with Elrond and with Gandalf, and here they lingered still in converse with their friends" (III, 325). But now we are coming close to the ending of the story, or rather, of this part of the story. It is not long until the hobbits return to find the garden at Bag End "full of huts and sheds, some so near the old westward windows that they cut off all their light" (III, 367)—Saruman's work. And then at the death of Saruman (III, 370), "about the body of Saruman a grey mist gathered, and rising slowly to a great height like smoke from a fire, as a pale shrouded figure it loomed over the Hill. For a moment it wavered, looking to the West; but out of the West came a cold wind, and it bent away, and with a sigh dissolved into nothing."

There is not much more to tell here. When Sam planted the small nut with a silver shale from Galadriel's box, there grew in the Party Field (III, 375), "the only *mallorn* west of the Mountains and east of the sea, and one of the finest in the world." And when Sam and Frodo ride out their last time together to meet the Elves, Frodo sings, "A day will come at last, when I / Shall take the hidden paths that run / West of the Moon, east of the Sun" (III,

381). And the Elves answer, "We still remember, we who dwell /
In this far land beneath the trees / The starlight on the Western
Seas" (III, 381). And when Frodo takes ship and "on the shores
of the Sea comes the end of our fellowship in Middle-earth" (III,
384), then "the ship went out into the High Sea and passed on
into the West"—"But to Sam the evening deepened to darkness as
he stood at the Haven; and as he looked at the grey sea he saw only
a shadow on the waters that was soon lost in the West."

Here we see again a linking of light and shadow with the west
(and east), though not perhaps as we would expect. Note that
from Saruman's view, and ours in Middle-earth, the westward windows of Bag End will let in light from the west, if not the West.
But when Sam is far westward of Bag End, at the Grey Havens at
the long Firth of Lune, then the ship bearing Frodo sails like a
shadow into the shadows of the West—not because the West is a
land of shadows but because the sailing is secret from all but the
Fellowship, as Sam and Frodo and the Elves pass unseen through
the Shire. There is no contradiction here—indeed Frodo carries
with him into the West Galadriel's light which comes from the
West. But this is a hidden path that runs East of the Moon, West
of the Sun, and the Starlight on the Western Seas is remembered,
not visible.

The wind blows from the West, blowing away the wrack of
Saruman's spirit as it has blown away the wrack of clouds above the
Field of Gorgoroth. The West is golden as the East is sapphire and
white. Summary will not do justice to the varying implications of
the West in *The Lord of the Rings*. We have set out much here in
detail, and yet, when all is said and done, there remains another
quest for us. Or at least a question. Is this simply a matter of detail?
Will summary not do justice because the act of summarizing will
eliminate necessary detail and connotation? Is there indeed an
underlying meaning to Tolkien's West, as we suggest there is to his
North? Is this West, as we have suggested, a Celtic West?

Because we (who have been reading these books for years) are
so used to the significance of Tolkien's West, and because we know
that Tolkien's mythology for England was designed to show that
fair elusive beauty that some call Celtic—and because, for me at
least, "Numinor" was the True West or ever I read Tolkien
(because I read of Numinor in C. S. Lewis's *That Hideous
Strength*)—it would be easy to speak of the significance of the West

in the Celtic world when we are really speaking of the significance of the West in *Tolkien's* "Celtic" world. It is advisable, I think, to examine a book from Tolkien's student days, to see what we can learn from it of the West in the Celtic world view, as it was understood then. The book is Thomas W. Rolleston's *Celtic Myths and Legends.*

Rolleston believed that there were three "Celtic" peoples: there were the autochthonous small dark pre-Celtic Megalith builders who brought the ancient religion from the south, who buried their dead, and who were "Celticized" by their Celtic compatriots or conquerors or overlords; there were the Celts of the plains, who burned their dead and who intermingled with the Megalith builders not through conquest but simply through settlement— and who may also have been "Celticized" rather than true Celts; and finally there were the Celts of the mountains, the "warlike Celts of ancient history" (57), who considered burning the dead a disgrace, the Celts of the bards and druids, "dauntlessly brave, fantastically chivalrous, keenly sensitive to the appeal of poetry, of music, and of speculative thought" (57). Of particular interest to us in our present inquiry is Rolleston's discussion of the Celtic "ship symbol" (most especially in burial sites)—which he connects, through the Megalith "Celts" to the "ship symbol" of Egypt and the doctrine of the Transmigration of Souls (71–84, 88–89).

The sun rises, of course, in the east and goes down into the west, bearing the day with it to the Western realms beneath the horizon or beyond the ocean. The "solar ship" marking at New Grange in Ireland (Rolleston 1911, 72) shows the sun, the ship, and passengers—as with certain Egyptian solar barks (75): one of these barks shows a single figure on a bier, while others are crowded with figures. The statement is clear. As the ship of the sun carries the day to the realms beyond, so it carries the dead (or sometimes the gods) to those same realms, with the day. The Egyptians (so far as we can tell) believed in the immortality of the soul, but also in its migration, or transmigration; the Celts (so far as we can tell) believed in the immortality of the soul, but also in its migration, or transmigration.

Because the final redaction of our Celtic stories comes from the far western edge of the Celtic lands, where—beyond Ireland the furthermost—is the sea, we find there a stronger linking than elsewhere of sea boats and the boats of the soul, and indeed between the sea and the sacred. In the story of Tuan, son of Starn, the brother of Portolan and the son of Sera, Tuan lives as a sea eagle all through the days of the Sons of Miled and the Tuatha De Danann, then as a salmon of the sea, until he becomes Tuan the son of Carell, and speaks to us in "The Legend of Tuan mac Carell" in *The Book of the Dun Cow* (Rolleston 1911, 97–101). So when the Elves and Gandalf and Gimli and Frodo and Sam take ship at the Havens and depart for the True West, they are the departed or the saints (like Brendan) journeying for Hy Breasaíl, the Sons of Don voyaging to the Summer Country, the men and ladies who sailed the soul—and they are in the right line from the ancient voyagers.

Or perhaps, if we accept Tolkien's chronology, the ancient voyagers are in the right line from them (a faint breath reaches even the late generations). It should be noted, however, that immortality is of the Elves, but the transmigration of souls of the autochthonous dwarves. And we might remark here, also, that the ancient (pre-Christian) Celtic beliefs and images linger in the Celtic stories of Christian saints.

Perhaps we should quote here from the rather Chestertonian lines of Tolkien's poem on St. Brendan ("Imram") published in *Time and Tide* in 1955 (I say Chestertonian, but there is at least— to me—a hint of Kipling. Or even of Walter de la Mare):

. . . When Shannon down to Lough Derg ran
under a rain-clad sky
Saint Brendan came to his journey's end
to find the grace to die.
'O tell me, father, for I love you well,
if you still have words for me,
of things strange in the remembering
in the long and lonely sea,
of islands by deep spells beguiled
where dwell the Elvenkind:
in seven long years the road to Heaven
or the Living Land you find?'

. . . .

'The Star? Why, I saw it high and far
at the parting of the ways,

a light on the edge of the Outer Night
beyond the Door of Days,
where the round world plunges steeply down,
but on the old road goes,
as an unseen bridge that on arches runs
to coasts that no man knows.'

. . . .

In Ireland over wood and mire
in the tower tall and grey
the knell of Clúain-ferta's bell
was tolling in green Galway,
Saint Brendan had come to his life's end
under a rain-clad sky,
journeying whence no ship returns;
and his bones in Ireland lie.

We are, of course, looking at *The Lord of the Rings*, and not at
later illuminations of Tolkien's meaning, but this is scarcely a
later illumination. I quote it because it places the Elves and the
sea and the ships and the Old Straight Road that are all part of
Tolkien's Middle-earth strictly in the context of Irish legend, and
at the very time he was publishing *The Lord of the Rings*. Or perhaps not quite in the context of Irish *legend*. It is worth noting
that when Rolleston (309–31) published an *imram*, he chose
"The Voyage of Maeldûn"—which is quite evidently legend—
from *The Book of the Dun Cow* (from the Whitley Stokes translation in the *Révue Celtique* in 1889), rather than the *Navigatio
Sancti Brendani*, which at least claims to be history. And Tolkien,
after all, is working in the realm of feigned history. In fact, in
choosing the story of Maeldûn, Rolleston specifically notes that
it tells "of adventures lying purely in regions of romance, and out
of earthly space and time" (309). But for all that, Ailill father of
Maeldûn came from the islands at the mouth of Galway Bay,
Maeldûn's voyage to Leix took him through the western islands,
and the island of the Monk of Tory (327–29) gave shelter to a
man of Donegal who voyaged in the western sea—so that even if
it was in a region of romance out of space and time, nonetheless
Maeldûn, like Brendan, voyaged in the west before he came back
eastward to Ireland.

The Celtic land of the dead in the west is the land of youth (in the west): it is not certain whether the ancient custom of laying graves in England east and west has to do with this (see Hazlitt 1905, 286ff). It may have to do with ships as coffins and their launching. There is a saint's life here that seems relevant. The saint in question (Cutha or Cuthbert), after his death, goes voyaging in his stone boat (coffin) for several centuries, with his body uncorrupted. He lives on an island where wheat (the grain of the living) will not grow, but barley will grow (the grain of the dead). It might even be profitable to compare his adventures to those of Brendan, if not of Maeldûn, though that will not be our task here.

Those who wish to study Tolkien's Northernness may have a more complex task than those who wish to study his Westernness— or, perhaps, his *Westernesse*. Hobbiton is in the North, though not so far as Norbury of the Kings. Northern rusticity is in part the subject of Tolkien's study in the *Transactions of the Philological Society* (1934) on the Northern "rim ram ruf by lettre"—but the whole Tolkienian attitude toward the North is to be found more through *Finn and Hengest*, and still more in Christopher Tolkien's edition of *The Saga of King Heidrek the Wise*, where the North also and especially preserves what has been lost elsewhere. The action of *The Lord of the Rings* indeed mostly takes place in the northwest corner of Europe, and has a British or English feel to it, though Gondor (home of the Sunnlendings) is well south of that northwest. Indeed, Tolkien wrote, in a letter to Charlotte and Dennis Plimmer of February 8, 1967:

> The action of the story takes place in the North-west of "Middle-earth," equivalent in latitude to the coastlands of Europe and the north shores of the Mediterranean. . . . If Hobbiton and Rivendell are taken (as intended) to be at about the latitude of Oxford, then Minas Tirith, about 620 miles south, is at about the latitude of Florence. The Mouths of Anduin and the ancient city of Pelargir are at about the latitude of ancient Troy. Auden has asserted that for me "the North is a sacred direction." That is not true. The North-west of Europe, where I (and most of my ancestors) have lived, has my affection, as a man's home should . . . but it is not "sacred," nor does it exhaust my affections. (Tolkien 1981, 376)

Of course, the sacred direction (if any) is the West. But the memory of the West is, in *The Lord of the Rings*, preserved in the North, as the memory of Gothic battles in *Heidrek's Saga*, and of Frisian days in *Finnsburh* and *Beowulf*. And as with the *sogür*, the preservation is factual—matter-of-fact—not Romantic. Of course, the North also preserves Evil, the Barrow-Wights, and Old Man Willow.

The North preserves what is lost elsewhere. I can see in the story of Arvedui Last-King the echoes of the polar expedition of Sir John Franklin, and the expeditions after him: they provide a good—indeed the best—Victorian example. In fact, one of the great stories of disaster in the North is that of the loss of Sir John Franklin, sent out with the *Erebus* and the *Terror* in 1845 and all trace of his expedition then lost for twelve years—when (in 1857–58) the record was found of his death in 1847 and the disastrous end of the expedition in 1848. In 1852, one of the more incompetently commanded of the various Franklin search expeditions (and the last mounted by the Admiralty), under Sir Edward Belcher, abandoned all four search ships including the *Resolute*, which made its own way out of the ice and sailed without guidance more than a thousand miles, where it was boarded by American whalers and sailed back to England (see Mowat 1973, 249ff). The Search for Sir John Franklin was a staple of Victorian news and current history, and a basis for novels and stories into the twentieth century. Ships lost in the ice and wrecks preserved in the ice entered the English consciousness in those years 1845–57, if not before.

Even more to the point, perhaps, is the role of the North in *The Saga of King Heidrek the Wise*. This is one of the *fornaldarsögur*, the Sagas of Ancient Times, and is in fact one of the class of *fornaldarsögur* based to some degree at least on older poetry, so that scattered throughout are references to ancient customs and practices of the pagan age (C. Tolkien 1955). The importance of this particular example of the *fornaldarsögur* to our investigation here may also lie in the form, in which the references to ancient customs are set out in verses inlaid in the prose—rather like what Tolkien has done in *The Lord of the Rings*. Be that as it may, we should look at the examples in *Heidrek* to see—as we will also with *Finn and Hengest*—just how strong and lasting this preservation may be.

The most significant of these preservations of ancient times is, I think, the "Battle of the Goths and the Huns" (though the riddles of Gestumblindi are at least a candidate for that title). Here are the opening lines of what is apparently a very ancient song or poem (45), far more ancient than *Heidrek the Wise*. "The pike has paid / by the pools of Grafá / for Heidrek's slaying / under Harvad-fells" (45). (This "Harvad" is an ancient Germanic form of the name that is now generally given as *Carpathian*.) And in the prose passage following there is the name *Danparstòðum*, clearly referring to the River Dnieper in Russia. Here, preserved in a Northern saga of the 1200s is a record of a battle in the Russian/Carpathian borderlands some eight centuries before. (It is worth remarking, I think, that the next reference to the Dnieper refers also to "hrís þat it mæra, / er Myrkviðr heitir"—the renowned forest that is named Mirkwood [49].)

Besides the Battle of the Goths and the Huns, and the riddles of Gestumblindi, *Heidrek the Wise* also preserves a description of the game of "Hnefatafl," clearly similar to *taflborð* and thus to the Welsh *Tawlbwrdd* (88). But this, though useful in corroboration for the preservation of old times in Northern memory (and as hinting at unguessed links between Welsh and Norse), is by no means significant in the same way as the battle and the riddles. Of course, this is not our only Northern preservation recorded in scholarly work, either from Professor Tolkien or from Christopher. In putting together for publication Professor Tolkien's *Finn and Hengest: The Fragment and the Episode*, Alan Bliss observed that his lectures on Finn and Hengest displayed "to a high degree the unique blend of philological erudition and poetic imagination which distinguished Tolkien from other scholars" (1983, v)—a unique blend directed, so to speak, at the question of the past—a past not from the North—embedded (even "alive") in a Northern text.

This entire book is a brilliant use of philological and linguistic analysis as an aid to history, though Bliss does suggest (as against Tolkien's view) that Hengest may have been a prince of the Angles rather than of the Jutes. But he accepts Tolkien's central arguments, based on the preserving text, (a) that there were Jutes on both sides of the fights at Finnsburh and elsewhere, and (b) that the Hengest of the conquest of Kent in England was the Hengest who fought at Finnsburh on the continent a few years earlier. This may all seem to be somewhat apart from our concerns here (though it is certainly relevant to the preserving North), but one point in any case should be emphasized. This book is a wonderful excursion into the world of the North, Beowulf, Finn, Hengest, Hnaef, Scyld Sceafing—even to considering Hamlet son of Earendil (this, admittedly, in the editor's appendix). But unless I have missed a few passages, the only ones *invoking* the North refer to the freezing of the northern seas (122) and the northern custom of fosterage (emphasized by the editor, p. 159, if not by Tolkien). The passage on the freezing is worth quoting, for Tolkien's tone.

> The function of this passage [ll. 1131ff] is two-fold: (1) Primary—the explanation of why Hengest (and company) did not sail away, at least as soon as their hurts were healed. . . . I take it they were capable of departing singly, or together. Winter prevented them, impassable storms, followed by the freezing of the northern waters: but spring came at last to end that winter, as it still does. (2) Secondary—doubtless . . . largely unconscious: a symbol or parallel to the moods of men, the winds to their troubled hearts, the ice to their forced inactivity . . . in a hostile land—the spring to the release of passions once more. (1983, 122)

I am reminded of John Buchan's great descriptions of the Canadian north in *Sick-Heart River*. What is important is that this is the North felt as part of one's own experience—internalized, we might say. In C. S. Lewis, for example, even in so deeply felt a passage as his description of his first reading of Tegner's *Drapa*, he recollects the pang of joy, but he is not (I think) exercising the Coleridgean feeling intellect that is at the heart of Tolkien's North. That is, Tolkien has internalized what the North means, the freezing, the daily struggle in small things, the matter-of-factness of the *sogūr*, the annual rebirth (in *The Lord of the Rings*, carried beyond as the rebirth even of an *Annus Mirabilis* and a whole New Age), the rocks and crags of Britannia's North. It is part of another story dear to him, of the English language, and another also—for did not Christ and his disciples speak with a Northern (Galilean) accent and provincial speech, but the kingship of Israel likewise was preserved there in the North, unseen for centuries?

And then there is Tolkien's great neglected 1934 essay on "Chaucer as Philologist." I am intending elsewhere to look more fully at that essay, particularly in the context of a kind of joint investigation of Chaucer by Tolkien, C. S. Lewis, and Nevill Coghill, in the early 1930s. Its importance here is that it illuminates, at the time of beginnings of *The Lord of the Rings*, Tolkien's understanding of the North as preserver of old forms and old words, but also the idea of separate development of forms in the North, of the sort later mentioned in the second part of appendix F in *The Lord of the Rings* (III, 513). There it is explained that it was "one of the peculiarities of Shire-usage that the deferential forms [of the second-person pronoun] had gone out of colloquial use. This was one of the things referred to when people of Gondor spoke of the strangeness of Hobbit-speech. Peregrin Took, in his first few days in Minas Tirith, used the familiar form to people of all ranks, including the Lord Denethor himself. This may have amused the aged Steward, but it must have astonished his servants" (III, 513–14).

As we noted at the beginning of this Chapter, it is in the appendices that we find more of the story and significance of the West set out (as well as of the North). It is also in the appendices that we find the end of this part of the story—whether in the Tale of Arwen and Aragorn (III, 428), or the end of the Tale of Years (III, 472), or one of the last notes in the *Red Book* (III, 451). It used to be argued, in Tolkien circles, in the young days of the 1960s, whether the last words of the story were "'Well, I'm back,' he said" (III, 385)—or "There at last, when the mallorn-leaves were falling, but spring had not yet come, she laid herself to rest upon Cerin Amroth; and there is her green grace, until the world is changed, and all the days of her life are utterly forgotten by men that come after, and elanor and niphredil bloom no more east of the sea" (III, 428)—or "Then Legolas built a grey ship in Ithilien, and sailed down Anduin and so over sea; and with him, it is said, went Gimli the Dwarf. And when that ship passed and end was come in Middle-earth of the Fellowship of the Ring" (III, 472).

In all these endings there is the fair elusive melancholy that some call Celtic, though I would say there is true Dickensian pathos only in "'Well, I'm back,' he said." ("Arter all, Samivel, she died.") If this is indeed the mythology for England of which Tolkien spoke—and it is—then the Celtic ambiguity by which the land of death is the land of youth, by which one voyages West in a stone coffin or a coracle or a ship of the sun, by which the immortal Elven ships and cloaks are grey with invisibility, is at its heart. The Tale of Years tolls like the Westron bell in the drowned lands, whether Lyonesse or Westernesse or Númenor of the great wave.

There is always the hinted melancholy of "Westron wind, when wilt thou blow?" Even the subtitle of the Tale of Years is "chronology of the westlands" (III, 452). But before we come to that Tale, we learn of Númenor and the *silmarilli*, and the three marriages of Elves and Men (III, 388ff).

Fëanor created the Three Jewels, the *Silmarilli*, which were stolen by Morgoth the Enemy and brought to Middle-earth, to his great fortress of Thangorodrim. The Eldar and Edaín fought against Thangorodrim and were utterly defeated. These Edaín were three peoples of Men, who coming first to the West of Middle-earth and the Great Sea, became allies of the Eldar against the Enemy. Idril of the hidden Elven city of Gondolin wed Huor of the House of Hador, the third House of the Edaín: their son was Eärendil the Mariner. He wedded Elwing, daughter of Dior, son of Lúthien Tinúviel (daughter of Thingol Greycloak of the Eldar and Melian of the Valar) and Beren of the First House of the Edaín. The sons of Eärendil and Elwing were Elros and Elrond, the Half-Elven. "Eärendil wedded Elwing, and with the powers of the *silmaril* passed the Shadows and came to the Uttermost West, and speaking as ambassador of both Elves and Men obtained the help by which Morgoth was overthrown" (III, 389).

For their sufferings against Morgoth, the Edaín were granted (by the Valar, the Guardians of the World), a land over sea to dwell in, removed from the dangers of Middle-earth. Most of them set sail over sea, therefore, to the Isle of Elenna, where they built Númenor, and whence they were forbidden to sail further West. The first King of Númenor was Elros, called Tar-Minyatur. The fourth King was Tar-Elendil, in whose reign the first ships of the Númenoreans came back to Middle-earth, and from whom descended the Lords of Andúnië in the west of the land. Tar-Elendil's daughter's son, Valandil was the first of these Lords, from whom descended Amandil Last-Lord and his son Elendil the Tall, who escaping from the wrack of Númenor with nine ships, was cast up on Middle-earth. "There they established in the North-west the Númenorean realms in exile, Arnor and Gondor" (III, 393). Through ten High Kings of Arnor, and fifteen Kings of Arthedain (ending with Arvedui Last-King), and sixteen Chieftains of the Dúnedain (Aragorn II being the sixteenth), the line of Elendil continued, and in it the line of Elros Tar-Minyatur, until at length Aragorn wedded Arwen, the daughter of Elrond, and the long-sundered branches of the Half-Elven were reunited. But both Aragorn and Arwen were of the blood of Tuor and Idril, and of Beren and Lúthien, and thus of Melian of the Valar. It could be said that as much of the West as was alive in Middle-earth came together at their wedding. The past walked in the present, the West as alive in the world, and that brought in the Fourth Age, in hope.

For with Tolkien, I think, even recapturing the past is a kind of advance. (Come to think of it, that is a theme in some of those writers with whom Tolkienian fantasy is connected—Kipling in *Puck of Pook's Hill* and *Rewards and Fairies*, and E. Nesbit in *The House of Arden*.) Learning the past is a kind of recapturing the past—Frodo and Sam grow through learning the past; in fact, it is only because of what they (and Bilbo) have learned, I believe, that they can come to Rivendell, and then to Lothlórien. But after the learning comes the true advance—Aragorn remembers, then takes, the Paths of the Dead, and then comes victory. The Ring cut by Isildur from Sauron's hand, bitten by Gollum from Frodo's hand, is destroyed because the Captains of the West knew the past, and because the line of the Kings (with Aragorn's knowledge, and his powers) was preserved in the North, so that in the Circles of the World, the Three Ages came full circle.

It is at the great set pieces in the narrative of the Great Days, the coming of Aragorn (III, 150), the overthrow of Sauron (III, 279–80), the coming of Arwen on Midsummer Eve (III, 309–10), that we see North and East and South and West laid out before us, in full—I might even say almost heraldic—significance. And we know that they are not accidental directions, but inherent in the very nature of the world's four corners. Perhaps from the boat that sailed the sun, perhaps from the ice of the north, perhaps from the hot blood of the south, but from whatever root, each has its sacral, if not its sacred, value. We need not go further into that—except perhaps to say that we who are the English-speaking inheritors of the World of the Rings will find our West going westward from England (and Ireland), our South going southward from England, our East going eastward from England. For the mind of this world is an English mind, the tongue our English tongue, the tale an English tale, and the trees are English trees.

5

Tolkien's Genius:
Mind, Tongue, Tale,
and Trees

We have thus far considered the tale, and especially its Edwardian antecedents and Edwardian mode; the study of tongues and its influence on *The Lord of the Rings;* the significance of North and West, and indeed of direction generally; and the theology of Tolkien's approach to the Incarnate Mind of this chapter's third epigraph, at the top of this page. Can we, in these four, find

Tolkien's particular genius and the reasons for the success of *The Lord of the Rings*? As the title of this chapter suggests, I believe there is one further reason, one further part of his genius, but that by and large these suffice. They may not be exactly coeval in Tolkien's development (though not far from it), but they are in the development of his creation. And whether we read the passage as describing how Tolkien himself went about his work, or (as I would prefer) we read it as discussing the universal process to which, *volens-nolens*, his own creation hewed, it still provides a key.

First, the Edwardian mode—the nature of the tale. The great exemplars of that mode—*She, King Solomon's Mines, The Lost World*—retain their popularity year in and year out, perhaps because of the adventures, but still more, I think, because of the mode. There is something very powerful in the image of the band of brothers abroad in the wide world, something very appealing in Tory England, something much attuned to our age in the idea of the past alive in the present, and something of great power in the commonplace narrator.

I once described the prevalence of Hobbits in *The Lord of the Rings* as an accidental goodness and took, as a result, a quantity of not-at-all-accidental ribbing from members of the University of Wisconsin Tolkien Society. It was of course accidental in at least one sense that the Hobbits, almost alone of Tolkien's creations for his children, strayed into his creation for himself (Carpenter 1977, 199ff). It was certainly a goodness, not only because Hobbits are the most ordinary of ordinary narrators, but chiefly for that reason. By a just instinct, Tolkien found his perfect plain men in the halflings.

Allan Quatermain, at least in Haggard's first books, is a plain, bluff man; a colonial, but very English in his character—English of those great days of Victoria's empire. Dr. John H. Watson, albeit (on some accounts) partly a colonial, is by consensus likewise a plain, bluff man and English of the English. Edward Dunn Malone is Irish of the Irish, but plain enough in that oddly assorted foursome in *The Lost World*. Even in the real-world antecedents of the Edwardian adventure story as I noted in the first chapter, we find plain Englishry (of the "pukka sahib" sort)—albeit sometimes, as with Stanley, raised to the theatricality of "Dr. Livingstone, I presume." It is evident that this is part of the appeal of the genre, or Stanley—that most complex of plain men—would not have arranged this case of life imitating art. But why is the ordinariness of the narrator important to the success of the narration? Is it because we are ordinary? I think not.

For the plain fact is that no one thinks of himself or herself as ordinary. In one sense, of course, "you have never talked to a mere mortal," but that is not what I mean. I think we put ourselves not on Watson's level—though surely in real life we should be over-joyed to achieve his dignity, selflessness, bravery, and love—but between him and Holmes. We see ourselves not as E. D. Malone but between him and Challenger or Lord John Roxton. Yet at the same time we are reassured by the narrator's ordinariness. If this can happen to Dr. Watson, why then, it could happen to us. If Holly can sit before Ayesha in Kôr, we might also. The narrator's plainness serves the function not of making us identify with him, but of reassuring us that this strange adventure really happened. That—paradoxically perhaps—is what the Hobbits do, and that is why this is an important part of the Edwardian mode. I do not know if earlier traveler's tales had this characteristic (was Sir John Mandeville a plain man?), but certainly it is highly important in the tales we are looking at here.

Of the past alive in the present, the more said, perhaps, the bet-ter. This is really (in the forests) the heart of Tolkien's world in *The Lord of the Rings*, as it is the heart of the Edwardian mode. It is, of course, a creation of the consciousness that the past differs from the present, and that the difference is not purely one of progress. The Middle Ages recognized that change is not necessarily progress, but they did not—as their art shows—realize that the past differed in any significant way from the present. Neither, for that matter, did the Renaissance. It is only with the coming of the Romantic view—the appreciation of the Gothic, Strawberry Hill, Beckford's Folly, Ann Radcliffe—and especially with Sir Walter Scott, that the difference is appreciated. With Scott it takes root in popular consciousness. Once there, it flowers rapidly. And it is still flowering.

The flowering can be seen in the whole set of beliefs in the occult that in the 1970s gave us *The Amityville Horror* and *The Omen* (fulfillment of prophecy being a special case). It can be seen in such staples of present-day (or at least very recent) fantasy as the Cthulhu Mythos. It can be seen in the search for our roots as well as in the anthropological approach to literature. All these appeal to the desire to have, or read about, the past alive or coming alive *now*. The phenomenon has something to do, I suppose, with the coming of the machines, with a perception that the Industrial Revolution was a kind of fall from grace. It is not, however, the same thing as that form of conservatism that sees us standing upon the shoulders of giants (from the past) or views the political process as a compact between past and present. The difference between the two is precisely that with the pygmies and giants, or with the compact, there is no discontinuity from age to age; with the "past alive in the present" there is.

This brings us, by a fairly direct path, to the idea of Tory Democracy. In the first chapter I suggested that Tolkien's Tory views, and those of the Edwardian Age, were drawing us afield from our concerns. By that I meant particularly that politics is neither the subject of stories in the Edwardian mode (barring some of Saki's) nor even very important to them. But then, Tory Democracy is not essentially a political doctrine, as those who have tried to practice it have found out. Winston Churchill may have been a Tory Democrat—that is, by way of definition, he believed in an alliance between aristocracy and squirearchy on the one hand and the people on the other. But he became Prime Minister only in that darkest hour when England did come together in fact. He is the exception that tests and defines (that is, "proves") the rule. Only in 1940, not even in 1945, could Tory Democracy "work" politically. Otherwise, we must accept the doctrine that, in essence, Toryism in any form is that political doctrine which avowedly prefers foxhunting to politics. As a form of Romanticism, based on a love of the land and a kind of longing for hierarchy, the relationship of master (say Frodo) and man (say Sam Gamgee), it is related to Chesterton's Distributism and thus to the same impulse that leads Americans back to the land on communes in Vermont. Nor is the communal aspect accidental.

For finally—and we might equally well use the nexus between Churchill and the Battle of Britain as our bridge—we come to the idea of the band of brothers, the final qualifying characteristic of the Edwardian mode. "Never have so many owed so much to so few" could serve as an epigraph for *The Lord of the Rings*. It could not serve for *King Solomon's Mines* or *The Lost World*, because those are essentially private adventures—a fact which should give *The Lord of the Rings* a substantial advantage over them in the public mind. But all these works have the appeal of the happy few.

This is not (and this must be made clear) the same thing as the appeal of the Inner Ring. We are not talking about the fellow professionals, the theme of so many of Kipling's stories from *Soldiers Three* on. We are not talking about unofficial hierarchies (as in *War and Peace*, to take Lewis's example) or about the strength of an appeal that can make men together do very bad things before they are individually very bad men. (This Lewis dealt with, in particular, in *That Hideous Strength*.) We are talking about the one sense in which *The Lord of the Rings* is certainly a quest—but I would rather say a "task"– narrative: the sense of great purpose that overshadows and ennobles the characters. Let me give a brief example of what I mean—not from Tolkien's works.

Consider the following chapter titles: "There Are Heroisms All Around Us"; "It's Just The Very Biggest Thing In The World"; "The Most Wonderful Things Have Happened"; "Those Were The Real Conquests"; "Our Eyes Have Seen Great Wonders." Without further knowledge, to what would we assume these belong? Certainly not to most of our present-day novels, nor to any novel of character. Perhaps to something like a pageant, perhaps even to an imitator of Tolkien, or perhaps (but here we may be led by their appearance in this context) to an adventure story in the Edwardian mode. They are, in fact, the titles to chapters 1, 4, 10, 14, and 15 of Conan Doyle's *The Lost World*, and there is about them that sense of purpose I mentioned above. It is especially important that it is "Our" rather than "Mine" eyes that have seen great wonders—a notable contrast for the twentieth-century age of anomie and alienation. (I cannot say what the twenty-first century will be, though I have elsewhere suggested that its characteristic fiction may be Tolkienian fantasy—in a paper delivered at the 2003 Hegeler-Carus Conference on the Arts in the Twenty-first Century and appearing in part in *The Rise of Tolkienian Fantasy*.)

For that sense of alienation, in the end, may be what explains the power of this image of the band of brothers. As we are increasingly set apart from our fellow men, we fall either into individualism in Tocqueville's old bad sense (into Bishop Bossuet's "every man his own church"), or into the heresy of confusing the Inner Ring, fashioned perhaps from a shared skill but existing largely for its own sake, with the band of brothers that exists for some great purpose. ("For he who fights with me today! Shall be my brother, be he ne'er so vile! This day shall gentle his condition"—a pleasant irony, perhaps, quoting Shakespeare to illuminate Tolkien.) In the United States today policemen call themselves brothers, as do African-Americans, but, for the most part, a sense of brotherhood is sadly lacking. This may be one reason for the widespread appeal of professional sports: fans otherwise sundered and separate are given the sense of belonging. (The theme song of the Pittsburgh Pirates two decades ago was "We Are Family," as the country came to know during their 1979 championship baseball season.)

Now it is to this need for belonging that the very idea of a company of heroes speaks. For all that Frodo and Sam are master and man, there are Nine Walkers, not two, and that fact, I would argue, is highly—perhaps transcendently—important for the book's appeal. Like the appeal of the past in the present, the appeal of the company comes from our rootlessness and alienation. I do not think it is because we identify with one member of the company and are comforted to find the others around us. Rather it is the very idea of the company that gives us comfort—and, indeed, "comfort" ("strength-with") is a highly appropriate word.

It is therefore particularly important that we never follow the adventures of a single figure for any significant length of time in *The Lord of the Rings*: even when we follow only one of the Walkers, he is with new companions. When Gandalf goes alone into the depths with the Balrog, we do not follow him. When Merry and Pippin are dressed as knights of Gondor and the Mark, that is the sign they have found new companions in their endeavor—not that they have left the old. This is a polyphonic narrative of companies, not of individuals: when Sam leaves Frodo it is a wrong choice in more ways than one.

This much Tolkien shares with his Edwardian peers. It is, as we have said, in the concern with language—in the philologist's world—that he parts company with them. It is here also that he parts company with much of the modern world. Our writers "indicate" rather than "say"; policemen in the Watergate case back in 1974 "responded" rather than "went" (or even "proceeded") to the floor where the break-in occurred; official Washington mushes through page upon page of regulations or announcements in bureaucratese, whose lack of style is matched only by its lack of clarity. I know of one economist whose English seemed particularly dense and who, when questioned, confided that he did not think in English but in computer symbols.

Do we miss this clarity in this style? We do. Even as we speak the gibberish we reject it, or are at least conscious of its insufficiency. We revenge ourselves upon it by finding beauty in the monosyllabic four-letter-word juvenility of street speech. To be sure, that speech is capable of both strength and accuracy, even poetry, but it rarely achieves it—achieving instead what have been called the dreary repetitions of the Orc-minded. In short, language currently (and for some time) seems to be approximating the exact contrary to the "speaking in tongues" of charismatic or pentecostal Christianity. Rather than seeming to be meaningless, but really having meaning, bureaucratese and gutter speech alike appear to have meaning but do not. No wonder we feel the lack.

Now whatever can be said of Tolkien's achievement, there is no question whatever that he uses words accurately and with unusual forethought, even on occasion with that pedantic accuracy which is in effect a play on words (the "Tale of Years"). We may sometimes sense a "Biblical" pastiche, but the same impulse that has led men to impute Biblical authority only to the "sacred English original"—to quote the story told by Dorothy L. Sayers—also leads us to welcome the familiar elevated diction and (possibly) rhythms. Whereas, a generation ago, the Bible and Shakespeare were only two constellations in a star-spangled sky of familiar great literature, these days the lights are going out all over the Western world, and even the Bible is more common in hotel rooms than in living rooms. (In a so-called New King James version, alas! that smoothes over any difficult meanings or phrases in the original.) But the memory lingers. A faint breath reaches even the late generations.

The naming and the language, then, are also part of Tolkien's appeal, though that is by way of being an accident. He may have set out to write an Edwardian adventure story (or a secondary epic following nature) when Allen & Unwin asked for a sequel to *The Hobbit*. He did not set out to appeal to our sense of the lost beauty and nobility of language; that appeal happened because of what he was. And he was as surprised by it as any. This is what we would expect of *genius* in the old sense; or, to put it another way, it is part of a sense of humor in the Muse. Be that as it may, one need only compare Tolkien's names with those of, say, E. R. Eddison (Lord Gro, Koshtra Pivrarcha) to see a naturalness in one, an appeal to an unremembered past perhaps, and in the other no more than a set of suggestive syllables. Yet Eddison was praised for his naming.

And the Incarnate Mind—the Mind of the Maker? We have drawn from *The Lord of the Rings* a familiar theology. We have seen a universe poised at a timeless moment different from ours, but in the same process of temptation. We have glimpsed the Holy Spirit abroad in Tolkien's world, and the gifts of the Spirit. We have looked in the Northwest of the Old World, and the pageant of the world's four corners. This is indeed part of our universe, and we can say that the Poet who uttered it through J. R. R. Tolkien is the Same through whose Word our world was made. Quite so. But in what way does this aid Tolkien's appeal?

There can be several ways of answering this question. We could say—Tolkien would himself say—that we recognize the Original Maker in the act of sub-creation. In the essay quoted at the outset of this chapter he has, in fact, said something very much like that. This we may call the theological answer. Or we could say that the timeless drama of temptation, the sense of great powers moving, the mixed familiarity and strangeness of what happens within us happening within the nations and peoples of Middle-earth, are what speaks to us—especially if we are reassured somehow by the presence of unfallen beings in the drama. This I might call a philosophical answer, and I suspect Tolkien would agree with it also. Or we might say that theological consistency imposes a particular character on any work of literature. That argument has been advanced by Miss Sayers in the essay quoted before; it may be called the literary answer, and it deserves elaboration here.

She made that point in the introduction to her series of radio plays on the life of Christ: "Except a man believe faithfully he cannot—at least his artistic soul cannot—be saved." Theological consistency, she was claiming (in defense of her own artistic endeavor), imposes a unity equal to, if not the same as, Aristotelian unity. Certainly the polyphonic narrative of *The Lord of the Rings* has unity neither of time, place, nor action: it is, after all, polyphonic. Nor—in comparison with *The Silmarillion*, for example—has it unity of language. Yet we perceive it as one work (at least most of us do), despite the publisher's expedient of making it a three-decker, despite the mutilation in the animated film, the slings and arrows of outrageous fortune hunting. (Of the present films I cannot say, without further time and thought, though they necessarily simplify and abbreviate—and thus falsify—the original.) Miss Sayers would have answered, as I say, that this unity we feel is theological. But what does that mean and how does it work? After all, most of us are close to being theological morons, either because we do not believe at all or because, having found God, we see no need for mapping His being. Theological consistency is not, on the face of it, something we value.

But we value *The Lord of the Rings*, and not least because we feel its unity. It is not merely that Men, Elves, Wizards, Dwarves, Hobbits, Ents, Orcs, and Trolls all act in character, though that in itself is part of this theological unity. After all, acting in character is part of many works of literary art. It is not merely that there is a sense of proportion, of part to part and of the parts to the whole. That also is true, and something of what Miss Sayers was talking about, but it is nothing like a full explanation. It is rather, I would argue, that this theological unity is itself mythopoetic. That is, the proper literary embodiment of theology is myth, or the creation of myth—*mythopoeisis*. Allegorical presentations, if they do not achieve myth, descend to mere personification, bearing to literature the same relation that mnemonic verses bear to poetry. That much has been noted. But it should be emphasized that myth is the natural result of theological concern, and especially that the more complete and consistent the theology the more perfect the myth. Let me make it clear that by *mythopoeisis* I do not mean, generally, fantasy in Tolkien's sense, but precisely the making of myth.

Perhaps the connection between mythmaking and theology has been most widely acknowledged in criticism of Melville's *Moby Dick*. Not only is the myth of the great sea creature a powerful one, particularly in the United States—witness the success of the movie *Jaws* in the 1970s or *Titanic* (for that too was a great sea creature) at the turn of our century—but, for *Moby Dick* at least, critics have almost universally asked questions exhibiting the theological implications of Ahab's search. Is the whale evil? Why is it white? Is Ahab a personification of some particular characteristic— vengeance, perhaps (but "'Vengeance is Mine,' saith the Lord")? Good questions, these, and nonetheless for having been asked so often. What has not been so often asked, and what I would like to discuss here, with *The Lord of the Rings* as my major example, is why myth and theology go together.

In part, of course, the answer has to do with a certain sweep—a certain breadth—implicit in both. But it has much more to do with the almost axiomatic fact that both myth and theology deal with gods. We may, to be sure, call them archetypes: we may Platonize them or Euhemerize them. The fact remains that the creatures of the myth simply *are*, without explanation, without character development. Asking why they are, and particularly asking why they are the way they are, brings us immediately into theology, rather than into literary criticism.

Suppose we ask why Gimli was not tempted by the Ring, whereas Galadriel (for example) was. The answer, I suggest, lies in the very fact that Dwarves generically might be expected to be tempted by the Ring as a *ring*, as a golden object, and this lower-level temptation would be theologically irrelevant—as though Adam had been tempted to eat the apple because he was hungry. Or suppose we ask why Galadriel *was* tempted? Tolkien has given us the answer to that question in *The Silmarillion*, and Christopher Tolkien has added to it in *Unfinished Tales*—and now in all *The History of Middle-earth*: the answer itself is not important, but the fact that the answer is theological is important—indeed, crucial.

As a Christian, I would of course argue that the truth of Christian theology leads to mythmaking more satisfactory than that based on any other theology—in other words, that the Mind of the Maker is incarnate here. But to do so would in our present discussion be a prime example of question begging. And in any case, mythmaking of any kind seems to appeal to our present age. Those who in the later 1970s observed books of "Jaws" jokes, stuffed sharks, and "Jaws" t-shirts and games can testify to that. Likewise those who have purchased *Titanic* memorabilia, or subscribe on the Internet to the *Encyclopedia Titanica*. Not to mention, at the beginning of the twenty-first century, all the panoply of Harry Potter products (and even those tied in to our myth of Middle-earth). Nor is it only our age: Fenimore Cooper's tales owed much of their popularity, I think, to their mythic quality.

Yet the theology implicit in *Jaws* is Pelagian if not Paleyite, though in a particular modern form of Pelagianism. (The shark is killed not by the Ahab figure or even by the academic expert on sharks, but by the apparently weak-kneed policeman who hates water.) The theology of Leatherstocking is Christian, though doubtless infected by those various heresies against which the first Timothy Dwight inveighed in his (and Cooper's) days at Yale: Natty Bumppo speaks not to the self-perfectibility of man but to his fall from natural grace. The fall from grace is, of course, the theological underpinning to the myth of the noble savage.

I would argue that it is the theology that captures the audience: we need to be told that our relation is to the scheme of things, to God or gods or the powers that be. But theology is not what the audience thinks is capturing it. What the audience perceives as its captor is the central mythic figure—the shark, Natty Bumppo, the Hobbit—and its element, its proper surroundings. For the shark, like Moby Dick (and here perhaps Jungian psychology could be used to illustrate our point), comes out of the depths of the sea, stirring (it may be) our racial memory. (And the great sea creature in *Titanic* went into the depths of the sea, almost like a returning.) And Leatherstocking strides through the depths of the forest; the key word here may likewise be *depths*. Tolkien himself has recounted his own reading of those tales: "Red Indians were better: there were bows and arrows . . . and strange languages, and glimpses of an archaic mode of life, and, above all, forests in such stories" (1984, 63). And what of Tolkien's own creation? The Hobbits would doubtless say if they said anything on the subject, that they were in their element at home in the Shire, and in one sense they would be right. But I know few readers to whom the chief appeal of *The Lord of the Rings* lies in the opening chapters, or even in the scouring of the Shire. The chief element in which the book functions—Hobbits and all—is the forested earth (and secondarily caves within that earth).

Elementary, you say—though perhaps not so many have seen it as should have—partly because the Hobbits have in a way strayed from another book, another set of stories, into the world of the Ents, the forests at the heart of *The Lord of the Rings*. In *The Silmarillion*, if I may be permitted the digression, Tolkien feigns that trees are the leaders, so to speak, of the vegetable kingdom, a point which could be deduced from *The Lord of the Rings* but which is not explicit there. We have already noted that trees can turn to evil, that they are sentient and capable of being tempted (on which, also, *The Silmarillion* provides further detail). They are, in short, characters in the story—but they and their forests are much more.

There were olden days when a squirrel could go from tree to tree across Middle-earth; Mirkwood and the Old Forest are relics of those days. The Galadrim are tree dwellers. The White Tree is the sign of the King's return. Even the Party Field in the Shire centers on a tree—first the Party Tree, then the mallorn. Mellÿrn also play a part in the elegy for Arwen and Aragorn ("There at last, when the mallorn-leaves were falling, but spring had not yet come . . ."). We need only look at *The Lord of the Rings* for the briefest of times to catch a vision of ancient forests, of trees like men walking, of leaves and sunlight, and of deep shadows.

But why is this world of forests so appealing? To that, there are at least three possible answers. First, it may be that forests are part of the Jungian memory. Second, it may be (as has certainly been suggested) that Tolkien's love of countryside and distrust of progress is in tune with our Aquarian age of ecology. Third, it may be that the first answer is unnecessarily profound, and the second unnecessarily restrictive and specific; perhaps we should say only that men love trees, and the "citification" of the Western world has made them more precious than ever. In other words, Tolkien's appeal to us may be Fenimore Cooper's appeal to Tolkien.

It may be the trees we love, or the tale, or the tongues, or the Incarnate Mind, or it may be all of these (as I think it is). But why is it Tolkien? Why did John Ronald Reuel Tolkien, of all people, create *The Lord of the Rings*? To some degree, we have answered that question, by looking at the years and reading of his youth, at his life's work, and at his life's belief. But other Christian philologists grew to manhood in Tolkien's generation. They may have read his creation with enjoyment, but they did not create it. They did not characteristically respond to a work of medieval literature by writing another in the same mode. They did not create Hobbits for their children. They may have written light verse or war poetry or books for children. If they were exactly of his generation they would surely have written war poetry or poetry after the mode of Rupert Brooke. But that poetry did not become part of a Silmarillion or a song of Middle-earth. What was the particular genius of this member of the King Edward's School Rugger XI, of the Tea Club, Barrovian Society, of the Lancashire Fusiiers (Lieutenant), of the OED and Leeds and the University of Oxford (D. Litt.), and the Order of the British Empire (Commander)?

One could answer, I suppose, that the *genius* attaches itself to the man as a kind of tutelary spirit. One could as well answer that the Muse strikes as she wills, not as we will. It is true. It has the form of an answer. But was it merely the Muse's jest to select Tolkien, a Hobbit himself, to create *The Lord of the Rings*? It was no jest. For the final thing we must note about *The Lord of the Rings* is that its success depends on the interplay of Hobbits and ancient world. Like Hobbits, we cannot live very long on the heights. We need rusticity amid our elevated diction, plain gardens amid our forests, inns amid our pleasures and palaces. And the answering of that need is what, in the end, defines Tolkien's genius. With all the other things he was—Edwardian, Tory (even if Tory Radical or Anarchist), philologist, Roman Catholic, Englishman of the Northwest of the Old World—he was, finally, and forever is, the image of Frodo Baggins. It was noted before that Hobbits strayed from stories he told his children into this greater story: it was noted that Hobbits are an accidental goodness. Just so, but the accident—the straying—was contrived by the Muse. Not in jest. In earnest.

Now the Hobbits, though self-portraits, are self-portraits drawn by the portraitist when he was forty (or more). The Elves, and most of the rest of *The Lord of the Rings*, have origins in Tolkien's youth. (The Ents, given that Treebeard's "Hoom, Hoom" is modeled on C. S. Lewis, are later.) The shift from the high style, the elevated diction, to quiet rusticity is partly a shift in viewpoint from youth to middle age, though Hobbits, like Tolkien himself, seem in many ways perennially youthful. This perennial youthfulness notwithstanding, and the frequent comparisons to children as well, the Hobbits are recognizably the creation of an older man. Had I wished to trespass further on Tolkien's private life, I could have discussed his four children, and his relationship with them; I have not, but the Hobbits are, in effect, from Tolkien as father—more than Edwardian, or philologist, or Catholic.

But, it will be objected, the comparisons to children are valid: the Hobbits are childlike (or childish). Yes, but they are not a child's or even a young man's creation. And in this fact lies, I believe, a part of the appeal of *The Lord of the Rings*. If the forests and Elves, the knights and ladies, and the "païens ont tort" call to morality, are all in tune with a youthful romanticism (of a medieval sort), the Hobbits are a kind of reassurance that this youthful romanticism, this version of Middle-earth, will continue to have meaning into our own middle age. Rather than the slow decline of youthful hopes, the wearing away of high ideals, the growing success of the world (along, perhaps, with the flesh and the devil), the cynicism and worldly wisdom of a creature accustomed to this fallen existence, there is implicit in *The Lord of the Rings* a promise. We are promised that within as well as beyond our workaday being there is high adventure, great peril, and the possibility of success in something other than worldly goods. We are assured that the Elven world we longed for is there—somewhere—however much we, like Tolkien, are Hobbits.

We seem to have come a long way from the Edwardian adventure story with which we started back in chapter 1. That pre-existing mode, apparently a slight and merely popular thing, is carrying a whole world for ballast and the Holy Ghost for mast—what have Rider Haggard and Conan Doyle to do with this? Even if we call it not an Edwardian adventure story but a particular kind of secondary epic following nature, its immediate literary forebear is still Haggard, and it is still in the Edwardian mode as we have defined it. At the beginning of this chapter we considered the peculiar appeal of this mode, and particularly that part of it we defined as "the past alive in the present." Could it be that this "adventure story in the Edwardian mode"—perhaps as a result of this characteristic—is in fact a far greater thing than we have believed it to be? I mentioned that its characters are types who sometimes (as with Holmes) rise to the dignity of archetypes. Could this be an indication that the Edwardian mode, whether we call it adventure story or epic, is mythopoetic?

Haggard was praised by C. S. Lewis as a mythmaker. Sherlock Holmes will live always in our minds at 221B Baker Street, with Mrs. Hudson below and Victoria on her throne. Is this perhaps part of the secret? Is *The Lord of the Rings* the apotheosis of something that was close to divinity before Tolkien began writing? Even Jeeves is a myth. Even Bertie Wooster. Have we mistaken the quality of the genre? Are we in a way rendering to Tolkien what is not peculiarly his?

For every action, the physicists tell us, there is an equal and opposite reaction. For the Industrial Revolution and the myth of progress that spawned or was spawned by it, there is a counterrevolution and a myth of anti-progress. For the story of man's perfectibility, the magic that makes dross into gold and men into gods, there is the story of man's fall, the black magic that has made dross out of gold and men into devils. But suppose, just suppose, a world in which Eden, though it must be striven for to be maintained, has never been lost. Suppose we have a myth of anti-progress recognizing that change may be ill, but not that it is inevitable. Suppose the contending forces are not the machines on the one hand and King Ludd on the other: suppose they are the machines and the countryside, Eden not at the confluence of the four rivers, nor whose gate is guarded by the angel with a flaming sword, but Eden in an English shire. Suppose it is not the new Jerusalem but, miraculously, something older than the old that is builded in England's green and pleasant land.

Am I trying to weave a spell? Perhaps I am. After all, weaving a spell is precisely what Tolkien has done, and it is not accidental that *spell* is the word both for "incantation" and for "story." Tolkien, by his imagined past, is liberating us from our present, and still more from a future we perceive and fear. We are not, of course, the Englishmen for whom he set out to provide a mythology. Nor are we the Inklings. Yet we hear what he is saying, for all that we may be overhearing it, and we respond with a quickening of spirit. Frodo lives, and we with him. England lives, and with it, us. But is England's green and pleasant land so powerful a myth within itself that it refreshes us?

The question that concludes this last paragraph, and the one about rendering to Tolkien what is not his alone, may be the same question in the end. The Edwardian mode is peculiarly English, indeed the Edwardian Age was peculiarly English, even when transferred (in the person of P. G. Wodehouse) to the environs of New York City. Why does this vision of England appeal? There will always be an England, but is that any reason it should be firmly engrafted in American hearts—not to mention the hearts of those Dutchmen, Swedes, Japanese, Romanians, and all who have read *The Lord of the Rings* in translation? The intersection of the timeless moment is England (for all that it is a country of the mind) and always (for all that it never happened). But why is this important?

"God gave all men a land to love"—thus Kipling in praise of Sussex by the sea. But Kipling was born and raised in India, and came to England from his exile. So also Tolkien came—but much younger—from his birthplace in South Africa. The contrast between the arid land around Bloemfontein and the green of England was one of his first memories. He was—to repeat a point made earlier—in England, loving England, but not of it. Since most of his enthusiastic readers are not of it either, that may be involved in his appeal to us. The question is whether another land could serve the purpose. Could the intersection of the timeless moment be France or Germany? Or must it be England? It must be—it is—in the Northwest of the Old World. Does that indeed mean England, only England?

Lewis, who was that most English of the non-English, an Ulsterman, would say yes, there is a particular spirit of England, different from the particular spirit of France or Germany. Even if that is true, why would this spirit of England be important to those who neither have seen the land nor descend from those who have lived in it? Tolkien's ancestry was English, as was Kipling's. Ours may not be.

But *languages* are the chief distinguishing marks of peoples. That is not merely something Sjéra Tomas Saemundsson said, or Tolkien repeated. It is not merely a key to Tolkien's critical doctrines or day-to-day belief. It is true, and *The Lord of the Rings* is evidence of its truth. I cannot speak for those who read it in translation, and I suspect that translators into non-Germanic languages, at least, will have substantial trouble with their task. But we who read it in English are, as English-speakers, the inheritors of Tolkien's English mythology, heirs through that grace of his kingdom. By the fact of our language, whatever our ancestry, we are native to that northwest corner of Europe that is the scene of *The Lord of the Rings*. The timeless has intersected our English-speaking lives at an English moment: because Sjéra Tomas's words are true, that moment belongs to us. *Si momentum requiris, circumspice.*

And that, but for some tying up of loose ends, concludes what I have to say here. The principal loose end has to do with the matter of temptation: is it somehow illegitimate for us to be invited to observe and even participate in the long process of temptation in an unfallen world? Does this not cheat us by making us think things are easier than they really are? Granted that *The Lord of the Rings* is theologically accurate, is it not psychologically "escapist" in this way at least? Fair questions, these—but it is the purpose of

Eucatastrophic stories to give hope, and the same theology that girds the world of *The Lord of the Rings* promises us that baptism overcomes original sin. In any case, Tolkien is not calling on us to take action, and his book is not a tract.

For we must be careful not to impute to a work of literary sub-creation the attributes of a Bible. Even if we find ourselves thinking in Tolkienian terms, using his characters and events to interpret our own lives, it is we who are doing this, not Tolkien, nor is he asking us to do it. During his life he accepted, even enjoyed, the efforts of his readers to apply to his sub-creation the same kind of scholarship he applied. He also strongly opposed those kinds of "scholarship" that looked at psychological journeys or involved any form of the personal heresy. He was a maker, not a psychologist, not even a priest.

This brings up a second loose end. I have from time to time, in what has gone before, explicitly rejected the use of *The Silmarillion* as a key to *The Lord of the Rings*. But Tolkien the maker made not only the one work, great though that is: he left many works, though this greatest among them. Why not look at them all? Why restrict oneself to this one work, when other parts might provide illumination (especially for chapter 3 of this book)? And especially when I have briefly looked at three or four of his scholarly works (counting his Imram). But these were at least scholarly works immediately available (except for *Language and Human Nature*, which was not and is not, because never written).

To this question about restricting ourselves to *The Lord of the Rings* there are two answers. First, I am specifically looking at *The Lord of the Rings*, partly because the continued success of most of the rest of Tolkien's oeuvre is derivative, partly because, when I first wrote this, I thought twenty-five years was long enough to wait for someone to spend a hundred pages or so seeing what it is that had become so popular. Second, so far as *The Silmarillion* in particular is concerned, there has not been a full reconciliation between that and *The Lord of the Rings*: not only are the tone and area of concern different (quite properly so), but on such things as the origin of the Orcs, one book must be wrong (presumably *The Lord of the Rings*) and one right. Either the Enemy bred the Orcs in mockery of the Elves (*The Lord of the Rings*) or he captured and perverted Elves (*The Silmarillion*), and even if we accept the capture theory, explaining away the statement in the earlier book, we are left with the fact that the Orcs in *The Lord of the Rings* do not sound like Elves in any way, shape, or form. Mockery perhaps, but perverted from Elves, I think not. (The film's attempt to reconcile these two versions seems to me off the point.)

There was in a letter to *National Review* during the Vietnam Conflict a description of the Eye of Sauron used as sign for our enemy in Vietnam. The writer suggested that *The Lord of the Rings* had become a lens through which the experience of the war in Vietnam could be viewed. That was, perhaps, an extreme case, but in the years since (and even before) there have been those for whom the World of the Rings lay in and around their own world. Sometimes in so derivative a form as Dungeons and Dragons. Sometimes now in images from the film. In a few cases, of course, because acting in the film together bred a fellowship not absolutely unlike the Fellowship of the Ring. I have noted that on one list-serv devoted to C. S. Lewis, many (perhaps most) of the communications at certain times recently have dealt not at all with Lewis, but with Tolkien. First, Lewis was the better known; then it was Tolkien. Then, over the years, it was Lewis again; now with the film it is Tolkien. And always, pre-eminently, for all the steady even sales of *The History of Middle-earth*, for all the instant sales of *The Silmarillion* back in 1977, for all the sales of *Mr. Bliss* and *Roverandom* and *The Father Christmas Letters* (in its various versions)—and even *The Hobbit*—it is *The Lord of the Rings* that is synonymous with John Ronald Reuel Tolkien.

In any event, we are here considering not Tolkien's appeal, or his achievement, in general, but in this one specific work, different in kind from all his others. This adventure story in the Edwardian mode. This philologist's story told by one for whom language defined human nature (and Elvish nature, and Orkish, and Dwarvish, among others). This Christian book whose timeless moment lives in a pre-Christian age. This story from the Northwest of the Old World that is forever England, and the Western Isles at the end of the Old Straight Road. This story from the World-Tree and the trees and forests of the world. This story from a world that has become so much part of my experience that I should like to write in it as well. This story also from a world not unlike that of the Celtic saints in the Northwest of the Old World in our timeline (and Tolkien's, who is my contemporary). All these and more, and I would like to give here some idea of the effect that

The Lord of the Rings has had on my life, serving as specimen where I may fail as a literary critic. Let me do so by telling you a story.

In 1967–8 there was a used-book store on State Street in Madison, Wisconsin, not far from the library. While I was browsing, I noticed a dog-eared card, posted on the bulletin board, advertising the University of Wisconsin Tolkien Society, and giving the name of its president, Richard West. I called him (he had, characteristically forgotten the very existence of the card on the bulletin board) and shortly thereafter went to a meeting of the society. In that society there was a community of spirit as well as of interest. From *The Lord of the Rings* grew friendship.

The word "grew" is important, of course, but more important was, and is, the friendship. C. S. Lewis, better than most, has described the growth and particular characteristics of friendship, using Tolkien as one of his examples. The critical characteristic is the shared interest, the critical moment its discovery. And if my own experience is representative, part of the appeal of *The Lord of the Rings* is not only that those who read and revel in it become friends from the moment of meeting, but that they feel themselves Tolkien's friends. This, doubtless, was hard on him: it cannot be easy to have millions of friends one has never met, especially when they call on one without warning or call one long distance in the middle of the night. Tolkien eventually went into seclusion to avoid the importunities of his admirers—which is itself testimony to the degree to which *The Lord of the Rings* caught them in its web.

The world has changed since those days. Tolkien no longer lives in Oxford, or indeed in the circles of this world. Conferences on Middle-earth no longer meet on Midwestern campuses. The long-awaited *Silmarillion*, though Tolkien himself failed to finish it, is awaited no more, and it has been followed by the *Book of Lost Tales* and thereafter by all the volumes of the *History of Middle-earth*. There is no longer a Tolkien Society of America, it having been folded into the Mythopoeic Society in California. *The Lord of the Rings* is no longer a discovery or even a cult book. It has, now in plain if not in full, been brought to the movie screen: that which we so greatly feared those long years past has come upon us—and not so ill done, some say, as we had feared.

But somewhere (and I do not apologize for borrowing these words) there is a corner of our mind where it is always 1966, with the Tolkiens at 76 Sandfield Road, and always the Great Years in the Third Age of Middle-earth. The timeless moment forever intersects our lives—both lives, in both times. "When Anodos looked through the door of the timeless, he brought back no message." But when John Ronald Reuel Tolkien looked through that door, he brought us back *The Lord of the Rings*.

In endless English comfort, by county-folk caressed,
I left the old three-decker at the Islands of the Blest.

—RUDYARD KIPLING, "The Three-Decker"

Afterword
From Third Age to Our Age

> *Now entertain conjecture of a time*
> *When creeping murmur and the poring dark*
> *Fills the wide vessel of the universe.*
> *From camp to camp, through the foul womb of night,*
> *The hum of either army stilly sounds,*
> *That the fixed sentinels almost receive*
> *The secret whispers of each other's watch.*
> *Fire answers fire . . .*
>
> —*Henry V (iv, chorus, 1ff)*
>
> *He that lives this day and comes safe home,*
> *Will stand a-tiptoe when this day is named, . . .*
> *Old men forget: yet all shall be forgot,*
> *But he'll remember with advantages*
> *What feats he did that day. Then shall our names,*
> *Familiar in his mouth as household words . . .*
> *Be in their flowing cups freshly remembered.*
>
> —*Henry V (iv, iii, 44ff)*

Tolkien's friend Lewis argued that the Great Divide in human history comes between the eighteenth century and ours, with the rise of the machines. What Tolkien thought of these machines can be seen in his strictures on the new mill in the Shire (though elsewhere, in *Mr Bliss*, he has fun with at least one of them). It is

115

perhaps ironic that it is the machines (films, computer games, DVDs) that have brought *The Lord of the Rings* ever more and more into the consciousness—the mind—of this age. This is not the place to set out a full discussion of Tolkien in our time (meaning, in this context, 2004): that will come, at least in part, in the last chapter of a book I am just now completing, *The Rise of Tolkienian Fantasy* (forthcoming, Open Court). Here, besides very briefly summarizing a few things I have to say in that chapter, I would like to concentrate on a sixth evident fact about Tolkien— a fact whose importance has only become fully apparent to me with Mr. Peter Jackson's film.

I have asked myself if there is any reason for my very mixed reaction to the film, besides Mr. Jackson's tampering with the story line (substituting Arwen for Glorfindel on the ride in the first film—or volume—or eliminating the Barrow Wights and Tom Bombadil). The answer is that there is almost too much action, and too much horror. Do not misunderstand me. Pretty much everything in the film was at least implicit in the book, and a filmmaker must follow his own conscience and taste in selecting what part of the story goes on the screen. But the fact is, Tolkien was a soldier—this is a soldier's book—and, moreover, he was a soldier in that war whose defining book was *Im Westen Nichts Neues* (*All Quiet on the Western Front*). To emphasize the great moments of action is almost necessarily to overemphasize them, and that may (necessarily) be what Mr. Jackson has done. Moreover, just as the Great War was a polyphonic narrative in our own twentieth-century history, so is *The Lord of the Rings* in Tolkien's feigned history, and some simplification of narrative (as well as the concentration on action) must be expected.

And yet it falsifies the nature of the soldier's story as it falsifies the nature of the soldier's life. Sam Gamgee is the good soldier, as Aragorn is the great commander, and Gandalf the wise counsellor, and Theoden the good general under the great commander. There are the scouting parties, the ceaseless patrols (we first really learn of them back in Bree with Strider), and a continuity with the great battles of long ago—almost as though Edward Creasey had been personally present at every one of his fifteen *Decisive Battles of the Western World*. But that's Victorian and this is 1915 (or '16 or '17). The women (Rosie Cotton, for example) are on the home front (except Éowyn, which is why the ride of a "battle-maiden"

Arwen is such a false step in the film). The fellowship is the male fellowship of battle. Merry and Pippin are the rankers who gain battlefield commissions. And of course, like most soldiers with their experience, like Tolkien himself, they are at heart pacifists, soldiering on, but saying in their hearts (with two great generals of the American Civil War) that "It is well that war is so terrible, or we should grow too fond of it," or that "They will tell you war is glory, boys, but war is all hell."

As we remarked earlier in this book, Tolkien wrote from words as his friend Lewis from pictures. In such a case, we, the readers, bring our own pictures—and for us, no one else's, not even Tolkien's (though his are appropriately and fortunately stylized), and certainly not Peter Jackson's, quite have it right. That is inevitable. But there is another kind of inevitability working here. Some years ago, Professor Shippey called our attention to the way in which Tolkien's etymological inspiration (so to speak) led him to "calque" his world on the myths of our world (1983, 77–8, 94–5, 97, 100, 144, 176–7, 182). By "calquing" he means the process by which the pieces of a compound word are translated bit by bit from one language into another, until a new word is formed—and by extension the process by which the elements of a compound world are translated until a new world is formed.

The French *haut-parleur* is "calqued" on the English *loud-speaker* (to take Shippey's example), and the Shire is "calqued" on England (77). I have suggested above that the adventure story in the Edwardian mode is by its nature mythopoetic, and this is certainly true of the Edwardian adventure story as story, printed or read—but not necessarily as film, which represents a different "calque." We speak sometimes of a "language" being calqued on the archetype or *mythos,* and I think of the use of *la langue* as a term in structuralist criticism. We might say that in *The Lord of the Rings* Tolkien translated the *langue* of his Middle-earth into the *langue* of our world (or calqued it upon that world), though he used almost all the *parôle* or story within that *langue,* in the process. In this case, we are defining the world, rather than the literary work, as the *langue.* Perhaps that is the way we distinguish *mythopoiesis* from other forms of literary creation, where the work is the *langue* and the sentences, not the patterns, are the *parôle.*

But see what happens when we come to the matter of film. Of course, Thornton Wilder has taught us the difficulty of dramatic presentation of fantasy, but a stage play (particularly Wilder or the Elizabethans) is at only one remove from straight narrative with quotation, while a film is further removed. Recall the dissolve from the wooden O to the vasty fields of France in Olivier's *Henry V*. And just as we have the huge background and history of Roland and Joinville and Froissart (in the English of Lord Berners) and Malory behind us in reading *The Lord of the Rings*, we have the epics of Francis Ford Coppola and Walter Wanger's *Joan of Arc*, and the Biblical epics (and *Ben Hur*) and John Wayne and a host of films from *Gone with the Wind* to *Saving Private Ryan* behind us when we see *The Lord of the Rings*. The world of the film is very different from Tolkien's world. Or, for that matter, Shakespeare's—which also had behind it Froissart and Berners and Malory.

Myself, if we were to have a film of *The Lord of the Rings*, I could have used a little more of *Le Grand Illusion* and *Im Westen Nichts Neues* and *The General* and *M*A*S*H*, and somewhat less Jason and Freddy—but we see through the lens of our own experience and our own life-history. And not only does Peter Jackson come to us from the world of horror films, but it is in any case very difficult for a film to represent the past alive in the present except as horror or terror. Rivendell remains in our mind and not so much our eyes. But, on the other hand, the *langue* of the film may be more suitable for *mythopoiesis* than the *langue* of the novel.

I suggest that it was absolutely necessary for the film to have come a half century after the book, for at least two reasons. First, when the book was first published, it was in the aftermath of the "Good War"—one might almost say, in the public mind, the unambiguous war—that is, World War II. But Tolkien's own war experience was far less unambiguous, more like ours in (let us say) Korea, if not Vietnam. (No, the Ring does not represent the atomic bomb or hydrogen bomb—they are merely a modern historical example of the greater truth that the Ring represents. It came before them.) We needed time to remember and reflect on the ambiguity. Only one thoroughly satisfactory "Good War" movie has ever been made—Olivier's *Henry V*—and even there is the weariness of "Upon the King" and the ruefulness of "And he'll remember with advantages." Weary and rueful—Frodo and Sam climbing through all that trench-war imagery of Mordor. The film had to wait, I think, until there was a point in reaffirming, however ruefully, the possibility—and still more the possible neces-sity—of the Good War. The reaffirmation comes more powerfully now. I will come back to this at the end of this afterword.

But there was another reason the film had to wait. Think of Led Zeppelin's "The Battle of Evermore," which is clearly Tolkienian, including even a reference to Mordor. Think of the most popular "rock" song ever recorded, "Stairway to Heaven," where to me there is a very strong Tolkienian light (shining perhaps through slightly maddened minds) in the figure of the May Queen, set in opposition to the lady who "thinks all that glitters is gold." (That line, of course, stands Tolkien's verse on Aragorn on its head.) In the 1970s the world of Tolkien's fantasy entered rock music and its much greater popular consciousness. So also, in the growth of Dungeons and Dragons, first as a role-playing game in person, then on the computer, Tolkien's world grows fixed in the popular mind. The writers who scripted Dungeons and Dragons—I learned at a Tolkien Conference in 1983—wrote their scripts as putative sequels to *The Lord of the Rings*.

From the fantasy of Led Zeppelin's "Stairway to Heaven" (and that was only twenty years after) to the rise of Dungeons and Dragons (also twenty years after) to the multivolume fantasy of Stephen King's Gunslinger series to the equally multivolume fan-tasy of J. K. Rowling's Harry Potter school stories (and Janet Rowling read Tolkien twenty years after), we can see around us the conquest of the novel—I might almost say, the conquest of our world—by that form of romance we call fantasy. Until Harry Potter, it would not have occurred to anyone to calque a mixture of Billy Bunter (or *Boys' Own Paper*) and *bildungsroman* on the world of (Tolkienian) fantasy—still less a further calque of the result onto the world of film. Now it virtually goes without saying or thinking.

Until the *Zeitgeist*—the Spirit of the Times—was wearing Gandalf's robes, we could not expect to find Gandalf on film (and not as an animated cartoon but in the form of a real Shakespearean actor). Above all, the idea of fantasy as war movie would have seemed—I think did seem—paradoxical or even oxy-moronic, until *The Lord of the Rings*. The film, it has been said, is the characteristic medium of the twentieth century. It may be, as I have elsewhere predicted, that fantasy in some interactive way, will be the characteristic literary form of the first half of the twenty-first. It is appropriate that the two should be joined at the cusp. But there is something more to be said here.

Something, I think, of Tolkien's popularity in the twentieth century (and now the twenty-first) comes from his participating in the breaking and remaking of reality as practiced by the Pre-Raphaelites and the Nonsense Writers in the nineteenth century. Lewis Carroll and his Alice achieved cult status in the 1960s. I know from my own experience that those who were Tolkien "fans" in the 1960s wrote *Leariste* limericks, loved the Alices, and even in some cases saw a seamless continuity between the Nonsense writers and *The Lord of the Rings*. And then there is this matter of pastoral. Tolkien may not have thought he was participating in the reconstruction of the ancient and obscure literary form of pastoral (William Empson's term)—his participation may have been an accidental goodness. But certainly the forests are the heart of Tolkien's world (he said so, or rather, told me that I was right when I said so), and if there is one thing more than another that has distinguished our last forty years from the time before, most especially in the United States, it is the growth of a generation that loves trees. (And of course, the Greenwood is always, in English literature, at least a little subversive.)

From pastoral to pilgrimage. The pilgrimage to the northward, to, or through, the barren lands—that also speaks (for whatever reason) to the mind and heart of the 1960s and '70s and '80s—and here the clearest example is in film rather than in fiction, in the various *Star Wars* films of George Lucas, and particularly in the first. In fact, it is possible that the wide popularity of certain books of science fiction on barren worlds, or in space, suggests they spoke in that same way to that mind and heart. (Would Frank Herbert's overpraised *Dune* be a case in point here, albeit for a different kind of barrenness?) But this is by way of being an aside—though, with *Star Wars* and its *mythopoiesis*, an important one. (And, if we had much more time, we might also consider the pilgrimage and *mythopoiesis* of *Star Trek*.)

Fundamentally, Tolkienian fantasy is indeed subversive: it seeks to remake reality. Or perhaps it would be better to say it *did* remake reality for tens of thousands of its readers. The Greenwood is subversive, likewise the horns of Elfland. Robin Hood's subversion. A Tory Democrat subversion, Cobbett's or even Blake's (but Blake was mad). I am reminded of Tolkien's remark when it was suggested to him that the literature of Faerie was escapist, and he asked who were they who most opposed escape, and answered himself, "the jailers." He is, like Henry Adams, by way of being a conservative Christian anarchist.

I mentioned the *Star Wars* films of George Lucas, and film is perhaps the best way in these days of breaking and remaking reality—bit by bit, frame by frame, a kind of paradise for new structural analysis. It has, of course, its own "reality" and its own conventions, its own world on which to calque our story, or its own implicit (almost necessary) form of story, its *mythos*, on which to calque our world. We have touched on that briefly, mentioning our war-movies. They, of course, differ from each other as war-stories (novels, books) differ from each other, as (for example) *The Red Badge of Courage* from *Miss Ravenel's Conversion*. Let us now, finally, look a little more at *The Lord of the Rings* as soldier's story. We may be surprised by what we find.

The first thing we should look at, perhaps, is that the soldier, in this case, was a volunteer, one who believed in his cause and who fought for an ideal. And one who did not become disillusioned with his ideal, no matter how much he may have with his war. A skeptic might say, well then, he must needs clothe his war-story as a fantasy, for in this world we will always become disillusioned. But Tolkien's world is our world, and what we said in chapter 5 applies here. The forests and Elves, the knights and ladies, and the "païens ont tort" call to morality, are all in tune with a youthful romanticism of a medieval sort, but in the Hobbits we are reassured that this youthful romanticism, this version of Middle-earth, will continue to have meaning beyond the war. There is, we might say, implicit in *The Lord of the Rings* a promise that within as well as beyond our workaday being, after as well as in the war, the Elven world we longed for is there—somewhere—however much we, like Tolkien, are Hobbits.

But then it is the fantasy (however we define that difficult word) that makes the Hobbits possible, along with the Elves, the Wizards, the Men of the West. The film necessarily makes the characters less extraordinary than they are in the book—there is no way to show the age of the Elves and certainly not of Arwen—and it turns out that it is easier to use the devices of horror rather than of awe to give a sense of incomprehensible things. But the fact that all the characters are recognizably manlike (humanlike) has the effect of bringing the wars of the Ring closer to our wars, of making this more rather than less a war-movie, and more rather than less evidently set in our own world.

With all this said, it seems as though the film—but not the book—answers our skepticism about war. Yes, war is terrible; yes, war is hell; yes, friends are killed or (like Frodo) maimed, and even those unwounded are unquiet in the heart. But yes, also, we few have stood a-tiptoe when our name was called, and our names, familiar in time's mouth as household words, shall remind those who come after, that for all the filth and death and death-in-life and treachery, all the fear, even terror, and the blackness of darkness, the dawn comes, there is peace a short while, and more than that, we have been on the right side. Victory is bittersweet, but this soldier's story at least ends in victory.

A citizen-soldier, in peace modest and humble, rising to meet the blast of war, as the hunting-men of the Great War tumbled over the top—and just so the Hobbits, citizen-soldiers of ages ago, rose to meet their challenge, in the northwest corner of the world that is forever England.

> *Once more into the breach, dear friends, once more;*
> *Or close the wall up with our English dead!*
> *In peace there's nothing so becomes a man*
> *But modest stillness and humility:*
> *But when the blast of war blows in our ears,*
> *Then imitate the action of the tiger;*
> *Siffen the sinews, summon up the blood,*
> *Disguise fair nature with hard-favoured rage . . .*
> *I see you stand like greyhounds in the slips,*
> *Straining upon the start. The game's afoot:*
> *Follow your spirit; and, upon this charge*
> *Cry God for Harry! England and Saint George!*
>
> *—Henry V (iii, i, 1ff)*

Appendix
A Sudden Coming, Being a Story of Later Time

> *Behold, I will send my messenger, and he shall prepare the
>   way before me;
> and the Lord, whom ye seek, shall suddenly come to his
>   temple . . .*
>
> —MALACHI
>
> *" . . . Don't the great tales never end?"*
> *"No, they never end as tales," said Frodo.*
>
> —J. R. R. TOLKIEN, *The Two Towers*

It was in the days after the king had died, the king who had come back from his exile to the city of the hill. On seven levels was the city, each delved into the hill, and about each was a wall, even in these times of peace, and in each wall there was a gate. Not in a straight line were these gates set, but so that in time of war the city might be defended, the paved way that climbed the hill to the great ship-prowed citadel wound this way and that from gate to gate. In these days of peace the gates were open, and men and women, boys and girls, might pass through. It was long by the count of men since the Great War, when the gates had been shut, with only men in the citadel and at the gates, and the women and girls sent out of the city for safety's sake.

In the years after the war, the great houses that had fallen toward ruin in the dark years had been repaired. The sounds of

men and their families were heard again in their halls and along
their broad pavements. The great carvings over their doors
were gilded again with fine gold. The warm sun picked out the
gold, and men forgot it had ever been said of old time, all that
is gold does not glitter. It glittered and glistered in the golden
sun.

On the day of which this story tells, a small company of boys
from one of the lower parts of the city, on holiday, had climbed the
way to the citadel and were looking down a thousand feet to the
valley below. One said to another—they disputed after who had
said and who had heard—that they should go into the great tower
of the citadel that housed the king's hall at its base, and a fair look-
out at its summit. And so they did, not secretly, for it was not forbidden, but quietly, in case one of the few guards might think it
forbidden, and hinder their going.

The hall of the kings was lit by deep windows along the great
aisles on either side, the aisles set off from the hall by rows of tall
pillars, greatly carved with beasts and leaves of elder times and
elder trees, bearing the wide vaulting above that gleamed with
gold, lately pointed, inset with bright colors. Silent between the
carven pillars were the effigies of kings long dead. Far at the end
of the hall was a dais raised many steps above the pavement of the
floor, on the dais a great throne, and above the throne a white
canopy of stone like a helm of the sea-kings of old.

No great meeting of the wise was held today, nor audience by
the king, and even the steward's chair on the lowest step glinted
black and empty. Meetings there were elsewhere in the citadel that
day, doubtless, but the hall was utterly silent, and the boys' minor
tumult and holiday silenced. So they went out swiftly and in confusion from the hall, and finding a door and a secret stair, climbed
to an attic room under the crest of the tower, none saying them
nay, for none saw them.

The attic room was cold stone, and narrow windows let in a
sunlight that seemed as cold, though the day was warm and the
sun golden without. The leader of the boys, braver and perhaps
more mischievous than the rest, cried out, but in a low voice lest
the stone echo, "A secret room! Surely in the great days great
things were done here in secret. I feel it in my bones."

And his lieutenant answered him, who was not so brave in his
manner, but better versed perchance in the legends of old, for he

came of a family of the wise, "In this room the great wrestled with spirits and foretold the future."

"Can you foretell the future?" the leader asked.

"In my family, among my uncles and great-uncles, are those who can. I have their blood."

"How do you do it?"

"We must come together all around the table and call upon a spirit. Are you game?"

To the leader it was as a dare in the schoolyard. He taunted those who would hold back, and slowly the young company gathered a little reluctantly at the ancient and single-chaired table in the center of the room. As they stood around the table, they were no taller than if they had been sitting, but the leader sat in the chair. Then he bade his lieutenant, "Tell me the words to use."

What he was told we do not know, for what happened after drove the words from his mind, nor can his lieutenant recall them. But slowly, as the words were spoken in that attic room, a dread grew upon those around the table. Each saw as in a dream, and heard as in the echo of a dream, mounds of men slain, and drums rolling wildly in the hills and rattling at the gates. The cold sunlight in the windows faded and a black cloud arose, and on that cloud and in it there was the shape of a horseman, tall, hooded, cloaked in black, crying aloud in a dreadful voice, speaking, in a tongue now forgotten of men, words of terror and power to rend both heart and stone. But it happened that though the lieutenant did not wish to speak, he continued speaking, and though the leader would have given all that was his not to repeat the words of the spell, yet he must repeat them. Even so, though the boys about the table would willingly have fled, they could not flee.

It grew so dark they fancied they could hold the darkness in their hands. Then each was aware he was watched, nor was it a friendly watch. Suddenly there shone in their midst a seeing stone, a dream and echo of the past and the dark years. They dared not look upon it, nor could they look away. But they did not see the future they looked for: they saw in its stead a writhing shape they cared not to see, in a pale flame. The flame glimmered out, and with it the shining stone. Then, in the pitch dark, they were conscious of a sleepless eye turned upon them, and a voice from whence none knew. "Who are these my servants who have called me?"

None answered, for all were dumb. The lieutenant had ceased his words of magic, and the leader's voice fallen still. Each of the company around the table thought of those things dear to him, green fields and sun and holiday, kin and kith, good adventure and feats of strength and arms, wrenched awry, marred and dishonored, befouled in the stink of the dark, and all the secrets of their hearts opened to that eye.

Yet it happened that one, not a braver but a dreamy lad, who it was said could forget his head were it not on his shoulders, fell out of the circle. Perhaps he was so wrapt in his dreams of good things that the Eye had less power over him. We do not know, but we know that he fell out, and the circle was broken. With its breaking the enchantment began to fail.

But it failed slowly, slowly, and as it failed, lightnings and the shriek of thunder rent the cloud. The doubt and great dread passed jaggedly away, that had hung in the room of stone, mocking the fair weather and clear sun without. Yet the leader and his lieutenant moved not, even when the door that had closed was thrust open, and the voice of the captain of the guard shouted out, "What is this here?"

None could form words to answer. The leader lay, head on table, as one dead. His lieutenant murmured a low crooning of self-pity. One of the lads, next to him who had fallen out, called endlessly, "the Eye, the Eye." And he who had fallen out babbled of green fields and forest and a secret place where he lay and dreamt sweet dreams, in the vale below the city. The captain feared to seize any, lest an evil be upon them, but at length he touched the leader and drew back his hand, saying to his men, "How comes he so cold?" Then he said again, "What is this? Speak!" But none spoke.

"Go. Fetch me a master from the houses of healing. There is evil and sickness in this room. See how the table here is scarred with a burning. Go!"

Two of his men went, down the long stair that none but they had descended in the days since the king was crowned. The dreamy lad began to rouse himself from his dream. "I do not know what happened, Sir. One minute they were calling up a spirit to foretell the future, and there was a light and a pale fire I did not care to look upon. I thought of my secret place in the vale, in those trees that are left there from the old forest, but in my thoughts all was dark, and fell things were about. Yet in them I called upon the lady of light, of whom I have dreamt there often, and then of a sudden I looked up, and there were lightnings in the room—I think they were in the room—and a rattle, of drums or thunder I knew not. What happened?"

"I do not know, lad, but look, one or two nearest you are stirring. Can you rouse them?"

He could not. "They are chill to my touch, like a serpent in sleep," he cried. The sound of men climbing the long stair was heard, and then there came into the room the master, summoned from the houses of healing, and they who had summoned him. He looked upon the leader, and then at his lieutenant. "Why, that is my nephew, my sister's son. What evil is this?"

His nephew answered not, but crooned his wordless song.

"Have you men enough to carry these all to the houses?" he asked the captain.

"I do."

"Then let us go, without delay, but hurry not too much on the stairs, for the dust of the years is on them, and the footing not good. Nevertheless, go not too slowly either. Time presses."

Each carrying his burden, with care, the men of the company of the captain of the guard went down the stairs and as the master directed, till they laid their burdens on the plain beds of the healers, skilled from the days of old in the healing of wound and hurt, and all such sickness as mortal men are heir to. Light the burdens were, too light, as if life had gone out of them, but it had not, though the leader and his lieutenant, the master's nephew, were perilously close to the door where mortal men pass but once.

The healers worked swiftly, not by magic but by lore, yet not all were roused from the cold into which they had fallen. But at length all but the leader and his lieutenant were sitting up, and the lieutenant at least had fallen silent, no longer crooning his wordless song. The master healer paused at the bed on which the leader lay, all mischief fled.

"He will die if no help comes. Go seek the king for our aid. All else fails."

It seemed an hour till the king came, though it was not. He asked, "What have we here, master healer?"

"A rash boy who has been carried from the secret room at the top of the stair long unused—a rash boy who trod the precincts of a room and a magic we would not dare to tread, and I fear with my nephew's help."

"We deemed that evil was ended for ever," the king said, "and yet it was not so."

In his hands he crushed the herb the master healer gave him, and its living freshness filled the room. The master healer's nephew sat up, then rose to his feet, and even the leader was roused, though not yet to standing or to speech. The master healer's nephew spoke at last.

"It is my fault, Sir. I gave him the words."

"What words are those?"

"Why, I do not know—I do not remember—I cannot say."

"That is well, Nephew. You will not be tempted to try them again. How came you to try them this time?"

"I dared him, and it is my fault. He did not know what I was daring, and I should have known."

"You were calling upon a spirit to foretell the tale of years to come, in the room where of old a greater man than all of us fell into destruction by that calling."

"I see, Sir. I did not know that. Should I have known?"

"No. Your ignorance can be excused, though not your action. But let us see to your friend. He has fallen again on his bed."

Again the king bruised the herb, and again the freshness awoke. All the others of the leader's young company were awake and abashed in the king's presence, but he drew breath as if wracked with pain, breathing shallowly and with long drawn-out gasps. Then again the freshness reached him, and finally he spoke.

"I am coming," he said, and then, "no—I am here—was it a dream?" And he fell back again.

"Third time throws best," the master healer said. A third time the king crushed the herb in his hands, and a third time the living freshness filled the wide room. The leader sat up, looking at what no man could see.

"What does the king command?" he asked, in a voice from beyond the years.

"The king commands a mischievous lad to remember where his mischief brought him. He also commands him to go home with his friends, and trouble us not more with his mischief."

"I will, my lord," the boy said, abashed. And then, in confusion, "I mean, I will go home, but I will not trouble you."

"The tale of the years to come is not to be told till the years are come, lad. And when you see a room where no one goes, and the warm sun shines cold through the windows, it would be best not to invoke what spirit has of old time cursed that room with his presence. You meant no more than mischief, but you might have brought upon us a mischance greater than any since the evil years, though that I do not know for sure. Go your way home, all of you," and then, looking at the dreamy lad, "save you. With you we would speak." For by now he had learned how this lad had fallen out and begun the breaking of the enchantment.

"How did it happen that you called upon the lady of light from the forest of old?"

"Since first I came to that wooded place in the fields where I have so often dreamt, my lord, I have known her, though I do not know her name. As the darkness rose and the shining and the pale fire entranced the others, I kept her before my closed eyes. I held her before my eyes to call upon her, though I could not call upon her by my voice, for as I say, I do not know her name."

"Do you not? Of what blood are you, lad?"

"That also I do not know."

"Have you no family?"

"I live with one who calls herself my great-aunt and may be. My father and mother I never knew, nor their father and mother, either of them. My great-grandsire perished in the days of the Great War, when the king returned. Of the generations between I know nothing."

"Give us your name and where you live, and go your way with the others, or if they have left, go your way home. I think you will catch them up." And so he gave his name and where he lived, and went on his way. Of that giving much happened, but that is another story for another time.

When he had gone, the king turned and spoke to the master healer. "There is evil still in the earth," he said. "That we knew, but we did not look for it to be called forth in mere mischief and by children. One could almost pity them."

"They were only playing, lads letting on to be men of great power, but there was real power about, and they ended by calling it in. They would perhaps have no just complaint if they were served as the king's enemies were served before, in the days of war when the power was abroad. For they knew all along that what they were doing was wrong. And yet, fell warrior though he be, the hands of the king are the hands of a healer, and after war and rumor of war comes the king's healing. Even for kittens who were letting on to be tigers."

"Will they take lasting harm? I would not that lads brave enough for such foolishness be maimed by it."

"I think not, nor are we harmed, but we must learn from their folly. Let us seal up that stair and that chamber. But more, we must not keep those of their age in darkness on great matters, well or ill, for after what is not known, dark though it be, will they always seek. That seems but footling advice after so stark a siege as we have here endured, like telling the storm-tossed mariner out of sight of land that he should keep his ropes well coiled and his weather-eye on the moon. But it is true for all that."

So the lads went their way back down the turning road from the prow-shaped citadel on the heights, and passed out through the great gate, and down to the vale below. The leader was loth to speak, and his lieutenant more loth, nor would the dreamy lad break the reverie in which he walked. But they three walked together companionably, and the others with them. Finally the leader spoke.

"I do not think I shall care to call spirits again, and I will not seek to learn the future, except by living into it. Was not the king good and gracious to us?"

"Do you suppose he will tell our parents?" one asked.

"Better my father keep his eye on me than that spirit I called forth" was the lieutenant's rejoinder.

"You called forth?" the leader said. "It was I who said the words. I called him forth." There was almost a touch of pride in his voice. But the dreamy lad finally spoke.

"You? No, not you nor any of us should be so evil as that. I hope we none of us have the desire truly to call that forth. I cannot say what is so for you, but the stink of its foulness still touches my nostrils, and if ever again I am in such a presence it will be too soon." And he went off among the trees, perchance to dream on his lady of light.

The leader and his company sat down in a circle on the grass, looking up at the city of the hill and the ship-prowed citadel at its mount. The sun lit the white stone and the gilded carvings on the seven levels of the city, for a thousand feet above the great gate, and a greater height above the vale. Nor was the sun cold, nor any stone, nor were there drums and shrieks and fell shapes in black cloud. There was peace upon the city and the vale.

And was there peace in the hearts of the young company? That I cannot say, and if I could, it would be to tell you another part of the story, or even another story. And that story neither could they foretell, nor at least then, sitting on the greensward in the vale, did they want to. Not then.

References

Aldiss, Brian, and David Wingrove. 1988. *Trillion Year Spree: The History of Science Fiction*. New York: Avon Books.

Blackwood, Algernon. 1929. *Strange Stories*. London: Heinemann.

Carpenter, Humphrey. 1977. *Tolkien: A Biography*. Boston: Houghton Mifflin.

Chesterton, G. K. 2001. *The Man Who Was Thursday: A Nightmare*. New York: Modern Library.

Crockett. S. R. 1899. *The Black Douglas*. London.

Haggard, H. Rider. n.d. [1888]. *She*. New York: Dover.

———. 2002. *King Solomon's Mines*. New York: Modern Library.

Hazzlitt, W. C. 1905. *Dictionary of Faiths and Folklore*. London.

Lewis, C. S. 1942. *A Preface to Paradise Lost*. Oxford, U.K.: Oxford University Press.

———. 1965. *That Hideous Strength*. New York: Macmillan.

———. 1993. *Letters*. Rev. ed. Edited by W. H. Lewis. San Diego: Harvest Books.

———. 1990 [1944]. *Perelandra: A Novel*. New York: Macmillan.

Lobdell, Jared, ed. 1975. *A Tolkien Compass*. Chicago: Open Court.

———, ed. 1980. *A Tolkien Compass*. New York: Ballantine.

———, ed. 2003. *A Tolkien Compass*. Chicago: Open Court.

———. Forthcoming. *The Rise of Tolkienian Fantasy*. Chicago: Open Court.

Mowat, Farley. 1973. *Ordeal by Ice: The Search for the Northwest Passage*. Toronto: McClelland and Stewart Ltd.

Pevsner, Nikolaus. 1954. *The Englishness of English Art*. London: Praeger.

Plank, Robert. 2003. "'The Scouring of the Shire': Tolkien's View of Fascism." In Lobdell, *A Tolkien Compass*, 105–113.

Rogers, Deborah Webster. 2003. "Everyclod and Everyhero: The Image of Man in Tolkien." In Lobdell, *A Tolkien Compass*, 67–73.

Rolleston, Thomas W. 1911. *Celtic Myths and Legends.* London.

Scheps, Walter. 1975. "The Fairy-tale Morality of *The Lord of the Rings.*" In Lobdell, *A Tolkien Compass.*

Shippey, Tom. 1983. *The Road to Middle-earth.* Boston: Houghton Mifflin.

Tolkien, Christopher, ed. 1955. Introduction to *The Saga of King Heidrek the Wise.* London: Nelson.

————, ed. 1984. *The Monsters and the Critics.* Boston: Houghton Mifflin.

Tolkien, J. R. R. 1934. "Chaucer as Philologist." *Transactions of the Philological Society,* 1–70.

————. 1954–55. *The Lord of the Rings.* 3 vols. Boston: Houghton Mifflin.

————. 1955. "Imram." *Time and Tide.*

————. 1965. *The Lord of the Rings.* 3 vols. New York: Ballantine.

————. 1981. *The Letters of J. R. R. Tolkien.* Edited by Humphrey Carpenter. Boston: Houghton Mifflin.

————. 1983. *Finn and Hengest: The Fragment and the Episode.* Edited by Alan Bliss. Boston: Houghton Mifflin.

————. 1984a. "English and Welsh." In Christopher Tolkien, ed., *The Monsters and the Critics.*

————. 1984. "On Fairy-Stories." In Christopher Tolkien, ed., *The Monsters and the Critics.*

West, Richard C. 1980. "The Interlace Structure of *The Lord of the Rings.*" In Lobdell, *A Tolkien Compass.*

Williams, Charles. 2003. *Detective Fiction Reviews 1930–1935.* Edited by Jared Lobdell. Jefferson, NC: McFarland & Company.

Wilson, Colin. 1974. *Tree by Tolkien.* Santa Barbara, CA: Capra Press.

Index